PHONE

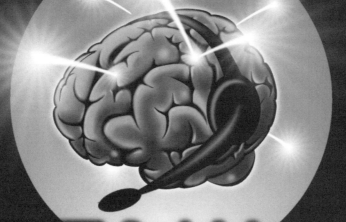

GENIUS

The Art of Non-visual Communication

– Michelle Mills-Porter –

Phone Genius

The Art of Non-visual Communication © Michelle Mills-Porter

ISBN 978-1-909116-26-9

Published in 2014 by SRA Books

The right of Michelle Mills-Porter to be identified as the author of this work has been asserted by her in accordance with the Copyright, Designs and Patents Act 1988.

A CIP record of this book is available from the British Library.

Printed in the UK by TJ International, Padstow

Jane,
lets crack these monsters!
Lots of love,
Micaela.
xxx

– Dedication –

To Mum and Dad, Henry and Tricia.
Thanks for your support and belief.
Love you.

To Mum and Dad number 2,
Cath and Elwyn.
Ditto!

And also for Stuart x

– Contents –

– Foreword –

In a time when communication methods are as readily available and as diverse as never before, the irony is that we feel less connected and are much less able to communicate with others than ever before.

In her new book, *Phone Genius*, Michelle Mills-Porter offers a unique insight into overcoming some of the shortfalls people have when using the telephone. Her years of experience in contacting senior people in a variety of companies and industries is testament to the skill she has developed in getting the right person, every time and time after time.

Following deep introspection, Michelle has identified and distilled what she knows and how she behaves and has crafted a formula for success on the telephone. She has taken what is natural, intuitive and second nature in her own communications process and offers it up in a succinct and entertaining text for us all to exploit.

For anyone that knows Michelle, you will hear her voice and personality come through loud and clear in the phrases she has spun. Those readers for whom Michelle is a new friend, you will be engaged with her talkative, frank and sometimes playful style. This approach does not detract from the key messages in this book. Indeed they add to the context and reflect the same positive state that Michelle recommends you adopt when you talk to people and, in particular, when using the telephone.

Predominantly a business book aimed at helping those that use the telephone to conduct their business, Michelle has actually crafted a book that demonstrates communications techniques that could benefit us all. One read is certainly not enough and it is undoubtedly a book that you will highlight and return to routinely to hone your communications skills and polish your telephone manner.

Martin Rhodes MSc MBA FCMI

– What people are saying –

'I have always admired people who are passionate about sharing knowledge. Whether as a speaker or an author, to put yourself out there with a genuine desire to help others be better at what they do is admirable.

What makes Michelle stand out in this very crowded 'business education' space is her ability to communicate her message in layman's terms and in a way that is effortless to learn. Her cheeky sense of humour helps also to keep you engaged.

Whether it's the telephone, Skype or Google Hangouts we cannot underestimate the impression we make to our customers and prospects. Building rapport and influencing an outcome over the phone will be made so much easier simply by following Michelle's advice. So, put the kettle on, find a comfy chair and enjoy!'

Warren Cass
Founder and CEO, Business Scene Membership Ltd

'Phone Genius is a gem of a course and book. It is more about the human being making calls than about the actual calls… and that, in my humble opinion is where there is greatest potential to make a noticeable and impactful difference. Michelle infuses her unique blend of magic into every aspect of this programme.'

Tony Burgess
Director, Academy of High Achievers Ltd

'Phone Genius courses are without doubt the best investment you can make if you want to really make the phone your friend. Invest in Michelle's knowledge. I had to make some really important calls and I practised what Michelle had taught. All the calls were a success and made without fear! Thank you, Michelle for sharing your knowledge. You are a credit to your industry.'

Gemma Taylor-Robinson

'Michelle is a top achiever. She was our source of getting appointments with key multiple retail groups and she delivered the results – appointments with decision makers who had been briefed on our market and were prepared to give us an audience. Her skills are valued highly and that is as it should be. What is even more impressive about Michelle is the positive mental attitude she exudes which attracts other people to her like moths to a flame! I am not surprised that she has written a book. If it shares a fraction of her telephone techniques to businesses like ours, it deserves to be a bestseller.'

Jonathan Ratcliff
Commercial Director, World Wide Magazine Distribution

– Chapter 1 –

Phone Genius – what is it?

Between the covers of this book lies the concentrated understanding of 25 years' experience of using the phone as a communication tool. It is the amalgamation of everything I have learned, developed and distilled. It contains the essence of all that I teach in my intense training courses, workshops and seminars.

Let's be clear: this is not a book on telesales techniques or sales strategies. *Phone Genius* is all about communication – communication at an evolved state, a higher level of consciousness, if you like. It explores how people who are great on the phone listen in a completely different way from those who aren't so good, and how they use their voices more effectively. It is called *Phone Genius* simply because I learned what I am going to share with you by using the phone as my main form of communication, but the contents are relevant wherever one person is trying to understand, and be understood by, another.

Yes, the contents of this book will enable you to be more effective in your communication over the phone, but the science spreads beyond that, and will enhance your communication skills in all situations.

I use the phone on a daily basis in my work winning new business for my clients, arranging meetings at director level, negotiating, selling, building rapport, networking and match-making. These skills, however, also spill over into all aspects of my life, as I was recently reminded when using them to get my Dad an appointment with a neurologist, and then into hospital when the time element was crucial. That sounds like a simple process, but in fact it took many difficult phone calls, and a need, on occasions, to impart a sense of urgency. Lots of negotiation and tenacity was required. Sometimes it was appropriate to be patient and calm, and at other times simply to express my exasperation. These elements, deployed in the right way at the right time, get you results.

Although the subject of communication undoubtedly starts with basic animal behaviour, and this is something we touch on, this book also explores the power of our intentions and how they can affect the results we achieve. It is, therefore, all about human communication at an advanced level.

I will use the word 'sales' in this book. This doesn't mean you have to be a sales person to take from this book, since we all have to sell ourselves, or our services, throughout the working day. Apply the contents to your situation, whatever it is, and use them in the way that is right for you. I use examples of reaching people in the corporate world because that's the clearest way to show the strategies I am sharing, but in actual fact these practices can be used in virtually any scenario.

The toolbox I have created in *Phone Genius* not only helps you achieve great communication on the phone; the tools you will learn to apply here can be used in all communication situations. They will take your skills to an advanced level, and will help you to communicate effectively whether or not you use the phone for the major part of your day.

These tools are also designed to be an asset to senior executives, such as key account managers, directors and business owners. Their time is valuable, and they need to be able to engage effectively on the phone at a senior level.

Communicating effectively sight unseen

There are two key elements that must be applied to everything I teach. They are: authenticity and personality.

If you can communicate authenticity and personality effectively over the phone, then you are more than halfway there. There are many lessons in this book that will help you to achieve this.

A long time ago, I found that using the phone to communicate meant to all intents and purposes stripping myself of the predominant sense that human beings use in communication – visual communication.

Working on the phone, I found that without sight, my other senses were enhanced and I could 'pick up' on things that others couldn't. I found that made me a better communicator in general, not only when I was using the phone. It wasn't long before I noticed that a lot of people who predominantly used the phone during their working day were far better communicators in general.

On the other hand, those who considered themselves to be great in face-to-face situations would squirm at the thought of using the phone instead. That is when I realised people need a very different skill-set in order to communicate effectively on the phone.

I've seen this in a whole range of situations. Take, for instance, sales reps who are forced to work in the office for a while and how reluctant they are to pick up the phone to reach their clients, or, Heaven forbid, to make their own sales appointments. Despite their stated objections that it is beneath them, or that they don't like talking on the phone, what it nearly always boils down to is a fear of failure. They lack the skills that those who communicate well on the phone have learned to develop.

I have never understood why sales people who work on the phone are less highly regarded than those who work 'on the road', despite the fact that they reach many more people in a fraction of the time. Salesmen are not selling while they are driving – just look at the expenses!

To communicate well on the phone requires an advanced skill-set that should be recognised.

What I have realised is that *only* without visual communication can we really bring our other senses to the enhanced level I am talking about.

Daniel Kish is the President of World Access for the Blind. He's blind and an astonishing human being who I will talk about further later. Daniel wrote this passage specifically for *Phone Genius* to corroborate the point that I am making:

'When I'm on stage, I read and respond to my audience by listening to every nuance that is happening – every movement, every fidget, every shuffle of every type of shoe, every yawn and turn of the head, every whisper, every stroke of pen to paper, no matter how many people or how large the auditorium – sometimes, even a smile causes the air to stir.

Yes, sometimes I miss things, but so do the eyes. The eyes see only what they are looking at. The ears can hear everything all around us, all at once. We just have to listen.'

That's quite beautiful and profound, is it not?

Ask yourself this question: Do you totally free yourself of the ability to see when you are on the phone, or do you try to visualise the person you are talking to? Do you try to picture the office, and the building? The reception desk?

Now, have you ever visited somebody with whom you have built a rapport on the phone only to be surprised or confused when you meet them? It's not surprising, is it?

The fact is, though, that many people who are great communicators over the phone never try to visualise the other person, so there is no break in rapport when they meet face to face.

I would like to start by telling you how I learned the elements of the subject.

I joined the Royal Air Force at the age of 17, and, when I left a few years later, I found myself with no trade, and no specific skill that was relevant in 'Civvy Street'. But, as I flicked through the 'Situations Vacant' pages of the papers, one thing became very clear. There were sales jobs everywhere!

It seemed to me that, if you could make it in sales, you would never be short of employment. They were well paid positions too, so I put in for quite a few of the jobs being advertised. I found myself being offered a number of possible options.

I chose a modest telesales position in a local magazine which sold advertising space, and quickly established that I was rather good at it. In fact, my first realisation of that was during the World Cup in 1990, when David Platt was the man of the moment. He had scored an amazing goal against Belgium, but the team had been knocked out, so they were coming home.

Our sales team was running a feature in which local businesses placed adverts in the paper to welcome the England Team home, and to say how proud of them we were.

Our promise was that we would get their messages to the team. I decided to see if I could actually get an interview with one of the squad in order to prove that our advertisers' good wishes had reached the players.

I was only 21, and John was a much older colleague. He had heard me trying to reach the secretary of England's manager, Bobby Robson to arrange an interview, and he thought it was ridiculous. Perhaps he was disappointed and bitter about his career; after all, he must have been in his forties, and he was still selling space for a very small magazine on a very low salary. Apparently the thought of our tiny little ads mag running an interview of any description was laughable, and he had decided to 'take me down a peg or two'. So I got a call back from Bobby Robson's office, and the man I spoke to was really enthusiastic.

'Michelle', he said, 'We really love the sentiment of what you are doing and we don't just have to do the written interview, we can get some TV cameras down to your offices and interview you on local TV too!'

I finished the conversation and put the phone down to squeals of excitement from the girls in the office. We were all thrilled! That was until John entered the office, doubled over in fits of laughter. It had been him on the phone, and he couldn't believe that I had fallen for it. I was crushed. What a horrible trick to play! I don't think anyone was very amused.

It was then that my physical education teacher's wise words came back to me. It was when I was playing hockey at school, and Miss Prest had said to me, 'Michelle, the best way to get revenge is to shut up, and stick one in the back of the net!'

So the incident with John gave me some serious motivation, and I was adamant that I was going to get the interview. And I did! A few phone calls later, and I had secured an exclusive interview with none other than my hero, David Platt!

There are several revelations here that are important to the whole concept of Phone Genius. The most powerful of all was the motivation. I had to get the result I wanted, and it wasn't down to sales skills, experience or practise. It was *mindset*!

Over the years, the importance of mindset and the power of intention has proved beyond a shadow of doubt that it has a bigger part to play in the results of your success than any other single factor.

Why should anyone still use the phone?

So, how much do we still use the phone for communication? Well, I think it is sad that we rely so heavily on e-mails and written social media. The massive pitfalls lying in wait for the unwary are already well documented, but, on a much less dramatic, day-to-day level, I see relationships damaged by misinterpreted e-mails all the time. I have been as guilty as the next person – I once lost a large commission cheque because of a misplaced exclamation mark! Smiley faces can be used, but they do not give much of an opportunity for expressing yourself – and there are quite a few people who find them inappropriate and irritating in business correspondence.

I recently read a heated discussion on LinkedIn in which somebody replied to a post which was written in capitals with the question, 'Why are you shouting at me?' Although it might have been intentional, it is more likely that the capitals had been left locked on by mistake, and the wrong impression had been given as a result.

Clearly, the issue is that the intended tone may be lost as soon as you press 'send', and you then have to rely upon the other party putting the correct interpretation on what you wrote. It's rarely accurate.

Using the phone is still a much more personal form of communication. In business, it is arguably the quickest and most effective route to reaching a potential client, and we can certainly control the intended tone much more accurately. It's true that we are using video and Skype so much more now, but technology has a fair way to catch up before it starts to help rather than hinder in this area.

It is said that effective communication can be broken down into three parts: vision (what you see), tone (how you say what you say), and words (the content of what you say). Many people already know that it is from the visual aspect of communication we draw most of our information.

Suppose, for instance, you encountered someone who greeted you with a face like thunder, and then said, in a slow, flat monotone, 'Hi, it's so great to see you, I've really missed you!' The incongruity would be very confusing. A mixture of all three aspects of communication factors will give you the best chance of reading the situation accurately, and of being understood as you intend.

Some people say they like to see the 'whites of your eyes' when doing business. To people who hold the opinion that modern-day communication has moved away from that, I say that my networking experience leads me to believe that it's making a comeback.

Given that the visual element is so important for most of us in our day-to-day communications, why on earth does the phone, which takes away the visual element, make you a better communicator?

First of all, it does seem to be the case that, if you lose one sense, your other senses become enhanced.

Daniel Kish, whom I made reference to earlier, is from California and is the President of World Access for the Blind. He is an expert in human echolocation, which has given blind people trained in the technique the ability to navigate using 'clicking' techniques. This is similar to the way in which a bat is able to detect obstacles in its flight path. Through their organisation, World Access for the Blind has trained more than 500 blind people in this technique. They are using subtle nuances in hearing to provide them with information normally provided by sight.

In my experience, people who use the phone frequently tend to be far more intuitive than those who rely upon face-to-face interaction. This is because their other senses have been enhanced, as they cannot rely upon the visual aspect of communication.

Imagine that you are trying to create a visual image, using only the spoken word. In order to do this successfully, you would have to be sure that your words evoke identical responses and images in the mind of your listener as they do in your own.

Well. You aren't both going to use the same words in the same way, with the same range of associations, all the time, are you? We don't even see colours as being the same a lot of the time.

We have a family joke about colour. I once asked my mother to indicate, on a paint colour brochure, where blue finished and green began for her. She indicated a point several shades away from my own choice, and did the same between purple and blue. Worse, when there was a family discussion on the colour of my nephew's blanket, opinions ranged from brown, to blue, to black – and there were only six of us in the debate!

The more people I asked, the more clear it became that we all have a different perception of colour. Of course we do! We are all individuals – and yet we assume that everyone else knows what we mean simply by hearing the words that we choose.

This is even more pronounced when we describe feelings. It is only when you ask somebody what they mean by a feeling that you gain a sense of what their 'word' means to them.

When we use the phone to communicate with others, these are the reasons that things can go wrong, and why we might not want to take the risk where business is concerned. This is particularly the case when technical or financial matters form part of the discussion.

Human beings are innately lazy, and I believe we have become lazy about our communication skills. As human beings, we have complex brains that have evolved in ways which allow us to modify our methods of communicating. In the world of phone communication, there are also new inventions for us to navigate our way through, such as voicemail. This is something I never used to have to contend with, and yet now it is an essential part of my training. There's also VoIP (Voice over Internet Protocol), Skype, satellite offices that put you through to other parts of the country, TPS (Telephone Privacy Service) and answering machines that don't allow communication with a real human being…

These are areas that we need to address when communicating on the phone, and yet very few of them are covered by any experts I know. This is why it is critical that people who are providing training in these areas are themselves actively engaged in using the phone to communicate, so that they are abreast of what's new at the sharp end.

This is another reason I was compelled to write this book!

– Chapter 2 –

What we all know about communication – and how we forget it!

Walter Freeman was the neurobiologist who stated, 'The cognitive guys think it's just impossible to keep throwing everything you have into the computation every time. But that is exactly what the brain does. Consciousness is about bringing your entire history to bear on your next step, your next breath, your next moment.'

So the human brain does record everything, and files it away. But the conscious mind and the subconscious mind are two different entities. I learned this in a very direct and personal way from my own experiences of PTSD and trauma following my involvement in the Asian tsunami. I also learned why hypnotherapy, which deals with the subconscious, can help to shift massive blockages, and so allow you to heal.

The ability to harness the extraordinary power of the subconscious is, as we will see, one of the skills that lies at the heart of effective communication.

Using our intuition

It was my friend Martin Rhodes, a very impressive coach with a decorated Forces background and rapier-like communication skills, who explained to me that it is the change to a group of nuclei in the brain called the basal ganglia, an organ responsible for a variety of different functions, which, in layman's terms, is responsible for collating all our experiences as data, creating patterns we recognise from any repeated experiences. It is also this area that flags up the anomalies we recognise as 'gut feeling', or 'intuition'.

Intuition is real and holistic. It is a product of all the data of all your experiences put together into one database, which is then drawn upon for every experience you encounter.

The sum of your experiences creates a body of evidence on which your beliefs are based, until the data changes significantly. Some 10,000 hours is needed to form a solid pattern you can rely upon.

Martin says:

Intuition has been bred into us. Our ancestors that made the intuitive leap from seeing a long dark shadow on the floor to 'It's a snake', survived a poisonous bite. Those ancestors that got curious and went too close got bitten and they perished along with their genes. By working with our mental physiology rather than against it, we bring our evolutionary strengths into play, and can generate some very impressive results. Remember, however, that intuition is but a part of a larger decision-making process. For bigger, more important decisions, learn to trust your intuition, but verify with other information sources.

Learning and the subconscious

We fail to follow our intuition at our peril. It has also been demonstrated that there is a huge role played by the subconscious mind in freeing the conscious mind to learn new things.

The most obvious example of this is learning to drive a car. This is quite a complicated task. The first time I sat in a car and looked at all the things I was meant to take on board and put together, I could not believe I would ever learn it all, nor could I understand how it was that most people find it easy!

People who are familiar with neurolinguistic programming will recognise the four stages of learning.

Subconsciously incompetent
Consciously incompetent
Consciously competent
Subconsciously competent

Before I ever sat in a car, I would have been subconsciously incompetent, meaning that I was unaware of what I didn't know. When I first sat in the driver's seat of that car, and looked at the controls, the gear lever, the pedals, the steering wheel, and I listened to the instructor, I was at the second stage, consciously incompetent.

After a few lessons, I could manage to drive, but I had to concentrate hard on everything I was doing. I was consciously competent.

A little while later, I did not have to think about the routine manoeuvres and controls, but I was certainly not an expert driver. I was becoming subconsciously competent.

Now, I can drive well. Everything is quite simple, and I do not have to concentrate, although my conscious mind does, of course, spring back into action should the unexpected occur! I am subconsciously competent, and I believe I am a good, safe driver even though I am listening to the radio or having a conversation with someone at the same time.

With such a routine task as driving home, we might realise that we have arrived home with no memory at all of the journey, and worry that we have been unconscious for the entire journey! In reality, it is only just that our conscious mind has been freed up as our subconscious does the driving.

My favourite television programme, *Horizon*, demonstrated this theory beautifully by using knitters in a brain scanner. Yes, that's right, knitters.

The demonstration was given by Dr Julien Doyon of The University of Montreal. Dr Doyon is the Scientific Director at the Functional Neuro-imaging Unit, University of Montreal. He carried out a brain scan on seasoned knitters, scanning their brain activity whilst they performed the stitches. This proved that a task that has been learned profoundly well can be performed automatically using the subconscious mind.

This is due to a phenomenon that neuroscientists refer to as neural plasticity which involves the way that new neural pathways grow, changing the very architecture of the brain and allowing the task to become automated. This is Dr Doyon's main area of expertise and he sent me this for inclusion in *Phone Genius*:

Depending on the complexity of the skill to be learned, it can take some 10,000 hours of performing a task before it can be done automatically but if you apply this to your own situations you may recognise some things that you do subconsciously.

This is worth noting. It means that you really can practise the elements of Phone Genius until they become habit. I encourage everyone to practise continually for 28 working days. If you do that for a start, and then continue to practise the elements beyond that, they have every chance of becoming habit and then, eventually, subconscious activities.

If you can understand your recipient's needs and wants before they tell you, you will build a massive rapport with them. When someone is intuitive about your needs, the feelings that can be evoked include trust and belief. You feel that the person is of a like mind, that they understand and care about you. We all want to be understood, don't we? We all want to engage with someone who has time for us, someone who cares about what we want. Therefore, these are some of the essential elements that guide people when they are deciding who they want to collaborate with, associate with, or even buy from.

Intuition can be developed, and it can give you a massive advantage in building rapport.

Someone once asked me whether developing your intuition could be considered manipulative, to which I have to answer, it's certainly advantageous to have a honed skill that allows you to understand someone a little better, but it can only be manipulative if your intent is to use your intuition to persuade a person to do something against their will. A person who does that would be a manipulator, regardless of their intuitiveness.

Blind sight

It was my favourite TV programme, *Horizon*, that also taught me about blind sight. Not only is it a fascinating subject in itself, but I feel it has a place in *Phone Genius*, as we are talking about communication without the use of sight. In the programme I watched, the Horizon team filmed a blind man while his ability to detect an object as it moved up and down was tested. The team checked whether or not he could 'see' the object to any degree, and he couldn't. However, when they conducted the experiment, he managed to detect the movement correctly 37 times out of 40.

What I learned from this experiment was that a small percentage of information goes directly to the superior colliculus or optic tectum. It is this that actually activates some eye movement and body movement. In my understanding, it is also this that directs the eyes towards a moving object. This is more prevalent in animals than in humans, because our frontal cortex is larger, which has reduced the size of some of the less-used areas of our brains.

In other species, the optic tectum is involved in a wide range of responses, including whole-body turns in a school of fish, or flocks of flying birds. The best example is, perhaps, those frogs or lizards that use tongue-strikes to catch their prey. So in effect, a small percentage of the brain is telling the eyes where to look before they see, not, as we might have imagined, their eyes getting the information first. Maybe there is a correlation, therefore, between scientific fact and what we might call intuition, or even psychic ability?

My own belief is that, when I am attuned to a higher level of consciousness (and it's not a constant state – for me it's more like catching a wave), it feels as if I am so intuitive that I am almost psychic. I am often amazed at my accuracy.

Examples of how this works during a phone call are explained further on in the book, but as a quick example, I sometimes say to someone on the phone that I have caught them in the middle of something and that maybe I should call them back another time.

They are always surprised at how I knew – and it's difficult for me to explain, as it always is when you do something automatically. I notice certain things that give me enough clues to make an assumption that will keep me ahead of the game. It has a lot to do with hearing what is going on in the background, or picking up little hints in their voices.

(There's more on this in the 'Listening Skills' section of the book in Chapter 10.)

Sales trainers of the 1980s might be getting palpitations in response to that example as I encouraged the other person to end the conversation with me. Like them, I was always taught not to give people the opportunity to say 'No', not to ask closed questions, but only to allow them to answer positively.

Nowadays, those kind of 'sales' techniques don't wash. I try to avoid any overly obvious 'techniques'.

The truth is that, when I tell someone that I have caught them at a bad time, the response is one of relief, or even gratitude. 'Oh, do you know,

Michelle, I didn't want to be rude, but yes, I'm really pressed for time at the moment. Would you mind calling back tomorrow afternoon?'

'Of course not, it would be my pleasure. What time is best for you? I'll put an alarm in my dairy.'

There are several things that have happened here; firstly they have happily given me permission to call back, so there will be no issue with getting through to them, which has effectively turned a 'cold call' into a 'warm call'; and secondly, I've firmed up the importance of the call by attaching a set date and time.

What else do we subconsciously bring to bear when communicating?

How do you soothe a crying baby?

'How do we soothe a crying baby?' is an example I love to discuss.

When I ask the question in a workshop environment I get all sorts of answers, most of which are right. There's movement, such as rocking our baby, gently swinging, even taking them for a short car ride. There's touch, such as stroking, or hugging. The way we use our voice in soft tones, 'Shhh'ing', or even singing a lullaby. Holding your baby next to your heartbeat is another great one. While these are all correct, what we are describing is secondary to the area I am trying to pinpoint.

In fact the first thing that we tend to do is subconscious.

We put ourselves into a calm state of mind.

If we alter our state of mind in order to create a feeling of calm, we then transfer that feeling of calm to the baby. You cannot expect a positive effect if you are in the wrong state of mind yourself.

Am I saying that babies pick up on our energy? Yes, I am. So this is where many people fall into two separate camps; either you will be thinking, 'Well, yes, of course, that's obvious!', or you will be thinking, 'OK, this is getting a bit fuzzy now.' I hope you're staying with me, because I intend to continue along these lines.

For me, it's animal instinct, it's one of the best examples of how we communicate as human beings, and we seem to brush over the fundamentals.

Animal whisperers

My favourite animal whisperer is the controversial Cesar Milan, the Dog Whisperer. In my opinion he totally understands dogs and their behaviour, what they need and what they want without anthropomorphising.

He talks about leadership and about asserting his dominance, but he doesn't do that through physical acts; in fact, almost everything he does uses state of mind, and communicating that state of mind, in order to achieve the desired outcome. I've heard a lot of people who don't agree with him, but he gets results, and from what I can see has a wonderful, mutually respectful relationship with his own dogs.

I also remember learning some invaluable skills from Barbara Woodhouse when I was just a kid. Although most people remember her for her motto 'No Bad Dogs', her autobiography *Talking to Animals* includes some of her extensive work with horses.

I remember seeing her on television, and being transfixed as I watched her approach a horse that was not used to her. She would walk towards it as it munched on hay, but when it looked up towards her she would stop, and then pretend to eat hay herself emulating, the horse's behaviour in order to gain acceptance. Then seeing her snort up a horse's nose, and gain immediate rapport and almost affection. To my ten-year-old mind, it looked like magic.

She was a pioneer in many ways, and it's widely accepted now that there are some people who communicate brilliantly with animals without necessarily using speech. It's certainly accepted that animals don't understand complex words, but they can understand tonality, and therefore commands.

I remember playing with my Nan's dog, Shep, as a child and finding immense pleasure from teasing her.

'Who's a smelly dog? Yes you are!' I'd say in an enthusiastic tone and gleefully watch her tail wagging. That must have been my earliest understanding of tonality overpowering words.

I did some lovely training with a friend of mine, Jude Jennison, in early 2012. Jude runs 'Leaders by Nature', and she holds a one-day training workshop that helps you to learn about your leadership skills using horses.

I won't spoil it by telling you what Jude does on her training days, but I will tell you that I started in such a tense state of mind that Jude's horse Kalle and I terrified each other. We were flinching at each other's every move. I had never been that close to a horse before, but I was hoping for a cathartic moment when man and beast made a significant connection. Perhaps it was disappointment when that didn't happen, or just my heightened state of anxiety, but I was so overwhelmed that my eyes started to leak! Yes, I cried! However, once I had released some of that anxiety, Kalle and I started making some real progress, and by the end of that day, with Jude's expert guidance, the breakthrough came, and it was a beautiful moment.

Again, in early 2013 I did another session with a horse called Mr Bojangles. He looked so calm and placid, I was eager to lead him around the arena, and I was confident that he would be compliant and happy. So I started off very confidently, and he followed me with no issue. Then he moved his head over to the other side of the rein, and then back again and there was an awkward moment when I wondered if I was leading him with enough certainty, and in that moment my confidence dropped.

I panicked a little, and negative thoughts rushed through my mind. 'Oh, it's not as easy as I thought! Is he going to play up? Nudge me? Bite me?', and he picked up on that immediately. In the next couple of moments he nudged me with his nose, and generally 'tousled' with me. I stopped.

I took a breath, re-focused and started again, this time firm in my thought process, and he followed me without too much of a problem. When we got back to the start position, my heart was racing, and Mr Bojangles didn't seem very happy. He was fidgety and kept throwing his head back and playing with his rein. Jude asked me how I felt, and I told her honestly. At this point someone else who was used to handling horses was at hand to hold his rein, but Mr Bojangles was still not settled.

Jude asked me to put one hand on his chest, near his heart and one on his back. She told me to try and match his heart rate, to lower my pace and feel calm. As soon as I did that, Mr Bojangles dropped his head and was completely at ease. My friend Drew Montague gasped and said, 'That was amazing!' and it was agreed that everyone saw a dramatic and instant change in the energy of both of us.

Again, it was such a powerful experience, and it proved to me that what we project is often what we want people to see, or what we aspire to be, but it's our subconscious that animals read. Humans are animals, too, so is it that ridiculous to believe we read on a subconscious level, as they do? That even though we colour it with language, posturing, body language, the authentic truth is held in the subconscious? That when we 'feel' uneasy with someone, it's not just 'gut instinct', but a sense of the subconscious truth? Mr Bojangles didn't care about the external show, he read my subconscious, and related to that.

This was particularly relevant for me, as I try to be as authentic as I can all the time, but sometimes it is necessary to check on whether the external show is totally congruent with the subconscious.

Of course, the external show helps us at times, when we want to appear confident when perhaps we are not, or when we want to appear calm when we are excited, but I find it really enlightening to explore the differences between our conscious and subconscious states. Also, that sometimes we have to encourage our subconscious to believe something, thus changing our 'state of mind'.

So when someone says, 'Don't show your fear' to a snarling dog, and you find yourself repeating, 'I'm not scared, I'm bigger than you!', you are in fact coaching your subconscious into projecting that message in addition to the external show.

If your message is not congruent with your state of mind, you won't be trusted or believed. If it is not authentic, then some people will read that.

Communication in plants

All right, so it's understandable when we are talking about communication between animals and people; after all, we're only a chromosome or two apart, aren't we? But what about communication in plants?

I believe it was during a David Attenborough programme that I learned about Acacia trees communicating with each other, but it may not have been. (I have to mention at this point that David Attenborough has to be my all-time hero! As soon as I hear his voice in a documentary, I'm transfixed!)

This is when I first came across bio-communication. I learned during this programme that when giraffes are browsing Acacia trees, they are put off after a while, and the conclusion was that the trees give off an unpleasant tasting chemical, very much like tannins. So the giraffe moves on, but tires of the next tree even more quickly.

It seems that the Acacia trees are communicating with each other to put off the giraffes. Now, I usually have some fun with this in my workshops, with people coming to all sorts of conclusions about how they do that, but, to cut to the chase, one conclusion suggests that it's only the trees downwind that pick up on the message.

If that is so, the tannins must somehow be transmitted in the breeze. As soon as the next tree picks them up, it starts to release the same tannins, which taste unpleasant to the giraffe.

I know that trees don't have noses, but, as I understand it, the chemical molecules are picked up by specialised receptors within the spongy mesophyll layer of the Acacia.

It is said that the tannins are released to help heal the tree where it has been wounded, but if that is so, why would the other trees start to produce the chemicals before they are injured?

The Secret Life of Plants (1973) is a book by Peter Tompkins and Christopher Bird. It was a best seller back in the 1970s. One of the book's claims is that, although plants don't have a brain or a nervous system, they still may be sentient. 'Sentience is the ability to feel, perceive, or be conscious, or to have subjective experiences.'

The subject of plant-to-insect communication and plant-to-plant communication was once dismissed by other scientists, and yet is now widely seen as being perfectly acceptable, with mountains of research to back it up.

Ian Baldwin was the pioneer, being one of the first in his field to investigate chemical signalling among plants in the wild, and Marcel Dickie and his team from the Netherlands did some excellent research in 1988, and as a result stated, 'The scientific community agrees that plants talking to their bodyguards is likely to be a characteristic of most, if not all, plant species. Even the gingko – a species that has been around for 150 million years – can communicate chemically with insects.'

Gary Vey is the Editor of viewzone.com which is currently read by more than one million people around the globe. Viewzone features articles about life and civilization, science, philosophy and controversies – views from different angles. He says, 'Our opinions are not always the popular ones but we encourage debate and opposing views and try to get to the truth.' This extract is taken from Viewzone with Gary's kind permission.

Can plants actually hear sound? This was the conclusion of Cleve Backster back in the 1960s. He's the former CIA interrogation specialist that connected polygraph sensors to plants and discovered that they reacted to harm (i.e. cutting their leaves) and even to harmful thoughts of humans in proximity to them.

Backster decided on impulse to attach his polygraph electrodes to the now-famous dracaena in his office, then water the plant and see if the leaves responded. Finding that the plant indeed reacted to this event, he decided to see what would happen if he threatened it, and formed in his mind the idea of lighting a match to the leaf where the electrodes were attached.

And that was when something happened that forever changed Baxter's life and ours. For the plant didn't wait for him to light the match. It reacted to his thoughts!

Through further research, Baxter found that it was his intent, and not merely the thought itself, that brought about this reaction.

He also discovered that plants were aware of each other, mourned the death of anything (even the bacteria killed when boiling water is poured down the drain), strongly disliked people who killed plants carelessly or even during scientific research, and fondly remembered and extended their energy out to the people who had grown and tended them, even when their 'friends' were far away in both time and space.

In fact, he found, plants can react 'in the moment' to events taking place thousands of miles away. And not only are they psychic, they also are prophetic, anticipating negative and positive events, including weather.

One of the most important things that Backster discovered was that, instead of going ballistic, plants that find themselves in the presence of overwhelming danger simply become catatonic! This phenomenon has posed endless problems for those researchers who, unlike Backster, do not respect the sentience of their subjects.

Under such circumstances, the plants they are studying evince no reaction whatsoever. They simply 'check out'.

Backster termed the plants' sensitivity to thoughts 'primary perception,' and first published his findings from the experiments in the International Journal of Parapsychology. His work was inspired by the research of Sir Jagadish Chandra Bose, who claimed to have discovered that playing certain kinds of music in the area where plants grew caused them to grow faster. Apparently this is true.

Another astonishing example of biocommunication is cordyceps, a genus of ascomycete fungi. There are more than four hundred identified species. Many of them use insects to distribute their spores by changing the host's behaviour – some of them in a most horrific way. Each cordycep fungi targets a different insect. Bullet ants, once affected by a cordycep fungus, will be slowly eaten from the inside out. The ant starts to hallucinate, and will start to climb a tree until it can no longer function. The fungus will carry on growing through the dead ant's brain and within three weeks will have grown a long fruiting shoot, from which it releases its spores. These spores will then burst onto the ground below, and start the whole process again.

Some fossilised leaves suggest that this process evolved more than 48 million years ago.

Biocommunication is a fascinating subject, and potentially raises many more questions, taking us in a totally different direction. After all, chemical communication is not going to help you when you are on the phone to someone in another country – but my aim here is to get us thinking about the different forms of communication, and allow us to open up our minds to what we do when we communicate using modern-day technology.

So let's get back to human communication and I want to ask you a very important question.

Why do you think we sound different on the phone?

– Chapter 3 –

Why do we sound different over the phone?

In fact, we can expand this question to take in all types of technology.

Take, for instance, a voicemail message that we have left on our own answering machine. Whenever I ask the question 'What does your voice sound like when you hear it back?' 99% of the room will cringe, and tell me that their voice sounds horrible and not like them at all.

Looking at this in more depth, most people say that their voice sounds childlike, higher pitched, or that they sound younger than they are. That is not what most people are trying to achieve when they are calling. It's often assumed that a higher voice indicates someone inexperienced or junior.

So what we can surmise is that in general we want to sound authoritative, knowledgeable and confident. These are things that are achieved with a deeper tone.

Often I'm told that people's accents sound broader on the phone, and almost every time I hear that people think they sound 'nasally'. Most people say they sound boring or monotonous.

In workshops I have played back delegates' voicemail messages, and the victims inevitably hide their faces and recoil. Yes, there are a few confident people who like their own voicemail messages, but usually those people will have practised the message several times before deciding on one they are happy with, and I can guarantee that they will also instinctively change their voices when they are on the phone.

So, what is the reason behind our voices sounding so different?

The Phone Monsters: what they do and why we must never forget them

It is as if there were evil beings lurking in the phone, stripping out all the tonality, all the subtlety of inflection, all the character from our voices, leaving us sounding flat, mechanical, robotic.

In my workshops I often refer to them as the Phone Monsters: Daddy Monster and Mummy Monster who seize all the living qualities in our voices and feed them to Baby Monster. This is what I imagine them to look like:

OK so you might think the Phone Monsters are a bit daft, but I tell you, they are a brilliant reminder to think about how your voice comes across on the phone, and I've often heard teams that I have trained reminding each other of their existence.

But, for those of you who want a more in-depth technical answer, here we go. It was my very good friend and trusted IT specialist, Jon Rixon (Lansalot Ltd) who helped me to understand this better.

Sound is a type of energy. It therefore works on waves, similar to light energy.

A sound wave is created when the air is moved backwards and forwards very quickly; how quickly is called the frequency and is measured in hertz – which means cycles per second.

We will get on to the more technical explanation in a moment, but in terms of overview, the phone takes our voice in analogue format and turns it into a digital format.

Analogue is undulating and fluid. The easiest example I can give is to ask you to picture a trombone playing a sliding note up and down.

In comparison, the digital version of our voice would be measured in square blocks. Let's say you play a middle C, from there you can go up or down in keys, even flats and sharps, but there is nothing in-between; you can only play the pre-defined specific notes of the piano.

Jon says, 'The change from our analogue voice into an electronic approximation of our voice (for transmission across the digital telephone system), and then conversion back again, means you lose some of your voice along the way.

Also the phone company can only transfer a finite amount of data down each cable at once, so if they can reduce the amount of data per call they can service more calls using the same cables. Data transfer is measured in kbps (kilobits per second) and for our purposes we just need to know that more kbps means better overall call quality.'

All this has an effect on our voice that makes us sound different on the phone. For instance, it cuts out most of the bass, making us sound higher pitched, or younger.

Jon told me that analogue lines have a maximum theoretical data bandwidth of around 56kbps.

In comparison, ISDN (Integrated Services Digital Network) lines have a constant guaranteed bandwidth of 64kbps per call, making them much better quality. This explains why the clarity of your phone conversations is so much better when you are on a good phone system using ISDN lines. A few months ago, this would have been my optimum choice.

However, I am using a VoIP phone at the moment from BP&N, and we are doing some work together. Voice over Internet Protocol (VoIP) is a technology in which voice calls are made using the Internet instead of normal telephone lines. This means that you can make significant savings on your phone bills by by-passing the telephone network.

I'm using a Plantronics headset, and I'm finding that, provided the broadband is good on both sides, the quality of the call is even better than a phone on an ISDN system. BP&N's Managing Director Rob Boylett says, 'Currently Voice over IP has come more into the fore and can run at 100kbps on g711 (this includes packet overheads) and therefore is theoretically the same clarity (if not better some would argue) as ISDN, which currently runs at a bandwidth of 64kbps per call making them a much better quality call than both a mobile or analogue call. You will notice a far better quality call on a digital phone system using ISDN lines or good hosted VoIP platform than over the traditional analogue line that only runs at 56kbps.'

Initially there were multiple problems with VoIP, including significant delays in between the transmission of your voice and the reply. Sometimes there was also crackling on the line and intermittent break up. I am still finding that when using my IP Phone, some people have problems hearing me, and I cannot tell why that is, although as I have 80mbps (megabits per second) broadband in my office, I suspect that it is the bandwidth their end causing the issue – something that will be solved in the near future with the general improvement of broadband speed.

My pet hate is talking on a mobile phone. Jon explained that mobiles have an estimated bandwidth of as little as 12.2kbps (there is an industry standard of 13.3kbps and some may go up to 20kpbs), and the very nature of wireless radio communications means they are sensitive to the environment – e.g. how far away you are from the transmitter.

Take a moment to think about all the times you have lost patience with someone just because the mobile signal kept cutting out. Tell me, how can you be in a rapport-building state when every other word is missing?

I'm going to talk briefly about body language here, and ask you what you think when you are communicating with someone who keeps hiding their mouth, or mumbling what they are saying.

Imagine you are buying a car, and the person you are buying it from is going through the service history. His hand keeps covering his mouth and you can't hear him clearly. Let's take it to the extreme: you are asking whether it has any problems, and again he is covering his mouth, so the answer comes back muffled.

Your instinct is to not trust his answer. Everything you know about body language, or even your own instinct, tells you that he is lying or covering something up.

Fact! There's no hiding from it! We are harsh animals and we make snap decisions. If you cannot be heard clearly over the phone people will not trust you! And worse, people will think you are lying. Why take that risk? Why put yourself in the position that you could break rapport with a potential client, or lose their confidence when negotiating just because they can't hear you properly?

Yes, we make snap decisions about people, and we make none faster than when we are on the phone, so I reiterate, if you want to communicate expertly on the phone, you have got to be better than those who do it face to face. It's a harder medium and a tough skill to master.

Jon likened talking on a mobile to watching a really old television compared to high definition. Why? Less information per call, per system, equals more money overall. They want to squash more people in so that they maximise their earnings.

The process of transferring your voice usually involves converting it into a digital sample in eight-bit resolution, or 8,000 sample per second. So in fact the technical explanation reflects the Phone Monsters. What happens to our voice is that the finer elements are stripped out and the inflections are dulled down, making us sound monotonous, and the bass is stripped from our voice.

We will go into this in more depth within the toolbox section under T for translation.

A good friend of mine, Neil Hillman, is a sound designer, re-recording mixer and location sound recordist with over 30 years' experience in recording the human voice for feature films, television programmes and commercials. He is also currently a PhD researcher, studying emotion in sound design at the University of York. He has this to add about the importance of clarity of speech in film, which has a direct relevance to the way in which we are judged when we use the telephone to make what we might consider to be a simple sales call:

> The human voice is special in film-making terms because it serves us humans as our primary form of communication. Therefore, it is a really important soundtrack element that needs to be carefully considered in any on-screen scene where people are actively interacting. Even if there is no dialogue present, it can have the effect of leaving an audience anticipating what might be about to be said.
>
> Now this absence of speech might be being used for effect, to build the interest of the scene or to establish a sense of suspense, or even to allow sonic space for the pictures and background sound to 'speak' and convey a message; but to my mind, the dialogue is the core

sound-element that everything else is wrapped around and effortless intelligibility is an essential starting point.

It might seem an obvious thing to say, but hearing a character speak very quickly establishes an impression of them in an audience's mind: through their accent (foreign, or regional), through social or cultural markers (are they an articulate speaker, suggesting a well-educated or affluent background, or are they talking the talk of the 'street-wise', the less well-off or less-privileged, or are they foreign and speaking a non-native language); through their tempo we can determine if they are calm or agitated, from their tone we might tell if they are nervous, confident, happy, or angry. We can even make assumptions about their health and lifestyle if for instance they have a 'gravelly' smoker or heavy drinker's voice. Is the voice old or young; high-pitched, masculine/effeminate and so on; all the specific things that an actor and director will work on when establishing a character at the read-throughs and pre-production stages will be understood in a moment when the character actually speaks.

It is worth remembering that all of this equally holds true for a salesperson following up a lead, as it does for an actor playing the lead. So, how clearly can you be heard? How high is the background noise when you make the call? How reverberant is the room you are talking in? How good is the quality of the telephone and the line you are talking on?

Here's the thing before you ring: the fastest way to lose a listener's attention to your message or call to action is to have them struggling to hear your every word.

Do that and you will break rapport!

– Chapter 4 –
The toolbox

So let's get cracking with the elements of Phone Genius. These four key elements are everything when communicating on the phone. They all feed into each other, and when we find ourselves facing a wall, it's one of these elements that will be holding us back.

The toolbox acronym is STOP!

Every time you pick up the phone to make an important call, a new introduction or several follow-up calls, STOP!

S	State of mind
T	Translation
O	Outcome
P	Positioning

S• State of mind

Your state of mind is vitally important when you call, because when you strip back to the elements of your voice it is harder to hide your feelings. If you are in the wrong state of mind things have a tendency to go wrong, or not to happen at all.

When I ran my marketing company, I could tell the type of day that my account managers would have well before the end of the day.

Inevitably, when I would ask the account manager who had a great state of mind what their day had been like, their reply would be really positive: 'Oh, great! I had some fabulous conversations, met some lovely new contacts, achieved some awesome results.'

Of course you did!

And to the person who was in the wrong state of mind: 'Oh horrible! Everyone I spoke with was really mean and no one wanted to listen to me, the product I'm offering is no good / the service I'm offering is no good / the contact list is no good...' You get the point.

But too many of us will fall into the trap of blaming our state of mind on what has happened. When we are making contact, it is we who are in control. We make the first move, so we set the mood. Easy to understand – a little harder to learn to master.

Practise it! If you set the tone of the conversation, then usually people react to you. If you smile or say 'Hello' to people on the way to work, what happens? You get lots of lovely interactions, and it sets you up for the day.

So why do we change when we put the phone to our ear?

If you are in the right state of mind, you are in control of the mood and the tone. If you take it to the extreme (I like to 'Kill them with kindness!' I'm not sure where I first heard that phrase, but it's so much fun to do!), it's really hard for someone to be in a bad mood.

There are some simple things that can affect your state of mind which relate to your environment. Heating is one subject especially for ladies. We have a slightly more sensitive response to variations in heat.

When I am working in the office for a lengthy period, I get very cold, and have to stop to run up and down the stairs a few times to get my circulation working again! It's the same thing if I haven't eaten for ages, or if I've worked through lunch. I realise I am very cold before I realise that I am hungry. Does being hot or cold affect your mood?

Maybe it's my Burmese blood, but I get utterly miserable when I am too cold; but then I'm really quite snappy when I get too hot, too. It can be difficult when you work in an office with lots of other people, but it's very easy to have a small air heater or desk fan that can provide you with a bit of relief if you are out of synch with the rest of the office.

Lighting can affect your state of mind too. I installed daylight lighting in the converted barns we used to work from. On top of that, I had lovely pleated blinds on all of the French doors and Velux windows, and sky blue and white voiles. The blinds were patterned like a blue sky with white fluffy clouds. Then, even on the gloomiest drizzly day, you could shut the blinds and the whole world still looked sunny and bright!

You can get light-saving daylight bulbs. Daylight bulbs make me feel happy; it's like the sun coming out. In comparison, I can't stand the fluorescent tubes that used to be standard in offices. You end up with eye strain, which gives you headaches, and the constant buzzing can really get annoying too.

I once worked in an office in Hindhead in Hampshire, just by the main A3 crossroads. It was a really bad bottle neck with traffic lights back then. The trucks and lorries waiting at the traffic lights would vibrate on a level that gave me motion sickness. Add that to the traffic fumes, and I felt sick almost every day. I wasn't at my best for communicating, to say the least.

In the same way, too much electrical interference can have an effect on your mindset. So just take a moment to check the fans on your computers. Check that things which don't need to be on are turned off, and ensure that you don't have any annoying little buzzing lights.

The number of environments I have walked into where people are working on the phone in the most unforgiving space! I've seen people crammed into corners behind filing cabinets. I've seen people working with their backs to forklift trucks, trying to raise their voices over the factory noise. I've seen people on their coffee breaks using all sorts of colourful language while the marketing guy is trying to make calls!

It's not rocket science, is it? We have to respect each other's environment, and create a little oasis that can allow your state of mind to be calm and happy, rather than uptight and stressed.

Think about this: when you receive a sales call, what are some of the things that annoy you? The same sales pitch being droned by a dozen people in the background of the call? A really bad quality phone line? The fact that they sound bored out of their wits!?!

We will go into more depth in all of these areas later, but for the moment, imagine being in what is commonly known as a 'Pig Pen', a telesales booth with a phone, a computer screen, piles of paperwork, and no photos allowed. How motivated are you going to be? How likely are you to be able to put yourself in the right state of mind, and to sound positive?

Now ensure that your office space has everything that you want in it. Do you have natural light (or daylight lights)? Do you have heating? Access to fresh air? Is there background noise?

I'm not encouraging anyone to be defeated if they are not in the right state of mind, but to learn to alter it. Give yourself the best chance by ensuring everything around you is helping.

I find that some people are really great at being able to change their state of mind in an instant, and Sybil from *Fawlty Towers* springs to mind. (*Fawlty Towers* was a BBC TV comedy first shown in the late 1970s but iconic to this day.) Sybil was the long-suffering wife of the insane hotel proprietor, Basil Fawlty. I'm sure she would have had an equal partnership, but she was front desk most of the time.

I can visualise her being on the receiving end of one of Basil's verbal tirades, and giving as good as she got back to him. Yet as soon as the phone rang she would pick it up and answer in the brightest of voices, as though everything were perfect.

I find myself doing that sometimes. I can be in the middle of making a stern complaint on one line, and when the other one rings, I can switch immediately, and change not only my tonality but my entire state of mind.

One thing that can help me to change my state of mind is a mood board. That's just a collage of things that I want to achieve, that I aspire to, places that I love going to.

It can be enough to remind me to crack on sometimes, and at best, can give me a real spring in my step.

If you really are stuck in a rut, then a quiet moment for some visualisation or meditation can work for some people. For my part, I prefer to get out of the place entirely, and take a walk down to the reservoir.

Just because it's fundamental doesn't mean it's unimportant.

I've never met anyone yet who can perform at their best when their heart is not in it, so don't skip through this point, take it seriously please. If you are not in the right state of mind, it will translate through your voice, and you are likely to damage your chances of building rapport with the recipient of your call.

The first point of changing practice is to learn to change your state of mind. Until it's mastered, choose another task.

Change Practice 1 – Change your state of mind.

Next in the toolbox is T.

T. Translation

What I mean by translation is the way we use our voice to translate our meaning.

In Sir David Attenborough's programme *Songsters*, he questions the evolutionary process which led to the human larynx developing into a complex, precise instrument. Although the programme is largely about song in all species, and how it is used to attract a mate, there is a lot we can draw from it, and apply to speech.

In humans, songs generate camaraderie and spiritual emotion. Elsewhere, in an excerpt from an interview, Sir David said, 'When I listen to a soprano sing a Handel aria with an astonishing coloratura from that particular larynx, I say to myself, there has to be a biological reason that was useful at some stage. The larynx of a human being did not evolve without having some function. And the only function I can see is sexual attraction.'

In the course of the programme, Sir David said, 'Shakespeare wondered if music was the food of love. Vocally, it was, and what is more, it still is.'

Think about the way that famous politicians use their voices to stir emotions; how speakers can motivate just with their voice; or how a girl can instantaneously 'fall in love' with a crooner... and, if we are open about it, how we find people's voices attractive even when they are just talking.

We can already build rapport, create relationships, and warm to people just with our speaking voices; however, by learning how we use them, we can also enhance their effectiveness.

It has certainly been beneficial to me to have learnt singing techniques, and to have been taught how to look after my voice. Your voice is the most powerful tool you have when communicating on the phone.

We have already discussed how and why our voices sound different when using the phone, but we have to compensate for the difference if we want to be perceived in the way we intend.

I was coaching a client a few months ago. He was really struggling with his business. He had boiled it down to the fact that he wasn't following up his VIP clients on the phone as much as he should, and when he was, he wasn't succeeding.

After a little time together we realised he wasn't making the calls because he was afraid of failure. And, guess what? As I suspected, the likelihood of failure was exacerbated by his state of mind. In fact, I will go so far as to say it was his state of mind that was showing itself through his voice.

He was unsure of himself, of his position as director of the organisation, sometimes he didn't feel worthy of it. He wanted to come across as assertive and sure of himself, but what happened when that doubting voice crept into his head was that he translated it subconsciously through his voice. 'Hi, it's Jonathan here at Brownings!' came out high pitched, jolly and, frankly, camp.

He sounded like a Red Coat from Butlins ringing to see if we wanted to come to the cocktail party that evening, rather than somebody who needed to check the financial statement prior to the auditor's review.

The truth was that Jonathan didn't feel worthy of his position, or confident in his ability to fulfil it. Of course, he had been chosen for that position for a good reason by his peers, and so my task was to help him to change his belief, and with it, his voice.

Now, you know when you're not happy and you start smiling in order to try and change your mood, and after a while it works? Well, you can do that with your voice, too. If you try to sound more confident, more authoritative, you often find that it makes you feel different inside. This can work both ways, and sometimes a bit from 'a' and a bit from 'b' can be the best mixture.

In this case, we worked on what we needed to do with the voice in order to make him reflect the persona he wanted; knowledgeable, confident and authoritative.

This is second nature to us, but let's remind ourselves of a few basics.

Some voice variations: high pitched, low tones, somber, jovial, fast paced, slow paced.

If you were chasing accounts payable for a seriously overdue amount, which of these would you apply?

And what if you were inviting a client to a party? Or calling to talk through a detailed proposal?

Let's explore further ways in which we can change our voice for different effects:

Inflection, tone, speed, volume, pitch, resonance, rhythm and timbre.

Bearing in mind the effect of the 'Phone Monsters', we need to ensure that we over-emphasise our inflections, and keep the conversation 'colourful'. That's highs, lows and changes in pitch, volume and rhythm.

There are three main elements to generating vocal sound. If you think of the human body as a set of bagpipes, the lungs are what give pressure and air flow to allow us to produce sound. Also in this area is the diaphragm, which is very important in supporting our voice, sustaining breath and controlling the length of a sentence, or note.

It's the voice box where the music is made (the larynx). Here, the vocal muscles and cords are responsible for developing the pulses that make the sound of our words, and that also change the pitch and tone.

Then you have the vocal articulators, which are everything around the mouth, including the tongue, cheeks, lips and palate.

These areas are largely responsible for the resonance of your voice in addition to the pronunciation.

I sang bass in ladies barbershop. In fact, my great grandfather was quite a famous bass singer, one of the first voices broadcast on BBC radio.

He was also a great conductor, and conducted many choirs around the Birmingham area, including the Cadbury Choir, Selly Park Ladies, Northfield Male Voice Choir, and the Birmingham Harmony Male Voice Choir.

I digress…

It was back in the 1990s, when I was in panto that the musical director suggested I had a *much* deeper voice bursting to get out. I was intrigued, and wondered if I'd inherited some of my great grandfather's musical genes. When I later found out that ladies could sing bass in barbershop I had to try it, and, as it happens, I was rather good!

When I was exploring my voice, I was fascinated by how you can change a note purely by altering your embouchure and the shape of your tongue. That's why professional singers pull such weird faces!

It amuses me to see great singers like Whitney Houston looking perfect when they sing, juddering their jaw to achieve a nice vibrato. The fact is that vibrato is achieved in the 'bag pipe' area, with your diaphragm, not in your mouth and although aesthetically pleasing on video, I would love to see the faces that great singers *really* pull when they are creating some of those magical notes.

It was when singing bass that I discovered much more about how to use the chambers of the body to change the sound of our voices: the chambers below in our chest cavity, and then the chambers around our vocal articulators.

Timbre can be the tone, the quality, or the emotion of a sound, and can be altered by the attitude you apply to it.

We can start to explore the use of our voices just by reading bedtime stories to our kids, or even reading poetry to ourselves.

We can choose how we want to sound, and practise it, and be aware of the way in which differences in our voices command different responses in others.

It's essential that we look after our voices, because they are our greatest tool on the phone. All of our muscles should be exercised like any other. Our voices should be warmed up and down when we have to use them for a period of time.

The very best vocal warm up exercise is to roll your Rs, or to hum if you can't do that. Start as low as you can and produce one long sliding scale going as high as you can and back down again in one breath. The more you practise this the further up and down the scale you will be able to go. When I do this in a workshop, people can physically feel their throats opening up after just a couple of attempts.

If ever you tire your voice, you will notice that it makes you feel totally exhausted all over. The best advice I was ever given was to *not* rest it. A bit like having a bad back, in most cases, gentle exercise is the best remedy. So, if your voice is tired or sore, continue talking, but just whisper instead.

I've noticed that, if I am speaking, and I don't have a quiet room in which to warm up my voice, rather than making a show of myself (or risk people thinking I'm a lunatic!), if I practise the exercises internally, that is, go through the motions but produce no sound, I can warm up my voice almost as effectively. Try it!

As well as exploring the timbre and range of your own voice, be aware of how the person you are talking to is speaking. Mirroring someone else's voice is a great rapport-building tool. Note: please do not mimic accents, it can be very offensive! What I'm talking about is matching volume and speed.

If you mismatch someone on the phone badly, they could easily not take your call, or even put the phone down.

The same goes for matching speed. If you want to build rapport, then you should try and match their speed. Try it the other way around and I guarantee that you will annoy someone. Do it with a friend who talks particularly slowly, and speed up when you are talking with them and watch the annoyance build.

Or take someone who talks really fast – really make an effort to slow down when talking and I bet they will try and speed you up, or finish your sentence for you. If you practise mirroring, you will find that you build rapport with others on a subconscious level.

> Change Practice 2 – Explore and practise getting colour into your voice and mirroring.

O. Outcome (desire, expectation)

In our toolbox 'O' stands for the outcome that you want, desire or expect, and it is incredibly powerful. This proves that your outcome is in your hands; in fact, it's in your mind. Something happens when we believe something to the core, when we are passionate about it and want to ignite others with it. It becomes infectious!

Others can get enthused, passionate, or moved by our belief, as if it's a tangible object that we are passing on, and yet this is achieved on the phone through our belief. That belief is translated through our voices. How?

To be honest, I don't know exactly. But, if we can understand how to put our mind in the right belief state, then the rest can happen whether we know how the voice is responding or not.

The best example I can bring to bear is when I was an account manager at Kalamazoo. I sold continuous stationery to the motor trade, and I loved it! I found that I was really good at it, and I smashed my targets even though others around me didn't. I was once set the challenge of achieving double my target in sales for three months running, and I did, for a grand reward.

I wanted to know what the difference was between what I was doing and what those around me were doing. I was one of the youngest, so it wasn't to do with age or experience.

It wasn't intelligence, as I certainly don't consider myself to be academically bright. And although I do consider myself emotionally intelligent, that wasn't a deciding factor.

Had I received more training than the others? No, in fact I had received less. Did I have a better database than the others? Well, one person did decide to claim that, and my boss at the time asked if I'd mind switching databases. I had built relationships with those contacts for ages, and it did annoy me, but to prove a point I went along with the plan, and guess what? Yes, I still continually broke my targets, and they continually failed.

It wasn't even attitude, as there were several team members who desperately wanted to be top of the leader board, and our attitudes didn't differ that much.

I spent a long time trying to understand what it was that I had been doing differently, and the only thing that I can honestly come up with relates to the order form.

This was back in the early 1990s, and we used a three-part carbonated order form, which we had to log into a register manually in order to cross-reference orders.

Every time I made a sale I would have to log the order number in the register and write out the order form. If for some reason that order was cancelled, we would have to also cancel it in the register. I envisaged that as the 'Walk of Shame' – my failure to secure a sale. Well, although everyone else only filled out an order form when they had made a sale, I often started to fill out an order form before I'd picked up the phone to the client.

I would fill in the company name and address details and the date. Sometimes I would even fill in what the order would be, WITH the commission I had made on the sale. We were allowed to add a margin to each sale of between 15% and 40%. Most might think that it was down to the negotiation with the client as to what percentage you could charge, but, being very creative, I offered all sorts of added benefits to increase the percentage of the commission, such as ghosting artwork into the paper, or selling the benefits of a higher grade.

So what was the point of writing out the order form before I had reached the client? Well, it was to set the outcome I wanted in my own head, which I found had an effect on my results.

Did it turn me into an aggressive salesperson? Certainly not, I've never made a hard sale in my life. My style is very much match-making, and finding a solution that suits the client.

What it did do was to make me try a little harder to reach the client, so when they were 'not answering at the moment', rather than just saying

I would call back, I would ask a further question; 'Do you know if they are out of the office, or just somewhere else in the building?' and if they said they didn't know, I would ask if they could please find out. I spent longer on the phone, but get this:

The extra time you spend on one call far outweighs the same amount of time divided between multiple calls in its effectiveness.

So 15 minutes spent on three calls will not be as effective as one 15-minute call. In fact, it's often the case that the longer you spend on one call the hotter it gets in terms of potency!

What it also did was make me try a little harder to find the right fit for the client, to find the right solution. This in turn made me a better salesperson on the whole, but it started with the outcome I wanted to achieve in that phone call.

What I realised is that setting the outcome we want to achieve translates through our voices, and changes the actions of the recipient.

Whether it is 'I'm going to sell some stationery to this company, I'm going to get an appointment, I'm going to get a customer care survey completed, I'm going to solve a complaint...' you must know what outcome you desire before you make the phone call.

It's great to think you can use your skills and fly by the seat of your pants when you're on the phone, but I tell you now, I have tested this time and time and time again, and if you decide what outcome you want to achieve first, you are at least ten times as likely to get it.

Why? Well it's back to that stuff that's hard to pinpoint: the confidence that you use guiding someone through a transaction makes you more believable, and more trustworthy. If you know where you are going, then people are happier to be led.

Of course, you could always try the opposite: 'I'm not going to get through to the person I need,' or 'they are going to tell me they are happy with their current arrangements.' Let's see how that works out for you?!!

This leads into the subject of positive mental attitude. There are many who subscribe to the fact that the universe will provide if you want it hard enough. Well, I know some people who truly want and richly deserve and the universe has not delivered for them, so I'm not ready to subscribe to that myself. What I do believe and have firm proof of, is that when you focus on what you want and think positively about it regularly, then sometimes, it happens.

How many of us write goals? Some of us do, some don't, but let me tell you about one of my experiences.

It was an incredibly surreal experience, a powerful and scary one regarding long-term goals. I believe it's the same principle at work.

I was sitting in my living room in Petersfield, Hampshire and I took a moment to look around me and take in how my life had changed in a matter of months. I looked at the gorgeous wooden floorboards in my rented bungalow. I was sitting on a sofa working from home, looking out through the French windows that opened up into the garden. My beloved cats were sitting nearby, I was on the best salary I had ever been on and I was incredibly happy.

It suddenly dawned on me that the written goals that I had prepared months ago were being ticked off in my mind. I decided to look up the goals that I had set maybe six months earlier.

Beautiful house… tick!

My ideal salary… tick!

Wooden floorboards and French doors that opened up into the garden… tick!… tick!

Working from home… tick!

My cats wandering round happily… tick!

Unless you had known that my life was very different just six months before, you might not have realised how significant this was.

It felt like the universe had provided, that the angels had dropped all of my wishes into my lap, but what I realised is the choices I had made to make these life changes.

As I thought back to how I got my ideal salary and how my new MD had told me that I didn't need the salary I was asking for, and I could get by on a little less for a short time until he could afford the increase. I had been firm. 'Sorry, no. I'm relocating, that's a lot of expense and a lot of risk.' We negotiated for ages, but I did not budge. That's how I ended up getting the salary I had put in my mind.

I remember that I had initially agreed on a different property but this one was advertised in the paper later. I remember viewing it and realising it was exactly what I wanted. Not only did I have to get out of my previous verbal agreement (which I did feel dreadful about), but I had to negotiate really hard for this property and the landlord had categorically said, 'No pets!' In the end, I offered to pay three months' rent in advance on top of what we had already agreed. I chased him gently, but daily, until he finally agreed.

The more I thought about it, the more I realised that everything I had achieved from my list of goals had been a result of the choices I had made. They didn't just happen, I had acted in accordance with reaching my goal on every occasion.

This hasn't just happened when writing goals, but also on other occasions where I have told my subconscious mind what it is that I want to achieve repeatedly. For me, it's the written word that is heard. So it's like my subconscious mind cannot hear me when I speak, but it can see through my eyes and it can read what I write. If my subconscious mind sees it, regularly, it will realign my decisions and my actions, so that I am constantly working towards the goals that I have set, even though I don't realise it consciously.

There are many ditties that remind us of this subject, such as, 'What you say will be the way.' But until you have experienced it, it must be difficult to believe. Whether it's angel wishes, tarot cards, faith, superstition or goal setting, I urge you to try to align your subconscious mind with your desires.

(I wished upon numerous shooting stars that my husband would fall in love with me and over 20 years later, it's still working!)

Anyway, that's long-term goals, but let's not forget the short-term outcome.

Change Practice 3 – Practise focusing on the outcome you want before you pick up the phone.
Ask yourself every time, what is it that I want to achieve?
And align your mind-set accordingly.

All of these elements in the toolbox feed back into themselves and complement each other.

The final element of the toolbox is:

P. Positioning

There are many uses of the word 'positioning', and they all have slightly different meanings. In marketing, positioning might mean something different to the branding term, or the sales term. So, to be clear what I mean by positioning, in this context it is being in the 'right and appropriate place', much like the dictionary's definition of the word.

Where are you coming from? Who are you? What gives you the right to pick up the phone and disturb someone else's day?

How can you change their life for the better? Why will they want to hear from you? What authority do you have that entitles you to advise them?

These are the sort of questions that you must have a bold answer for before you are ready to proactively generate new relationships on the phone.

It is very closely linked with your belief, and I will state very firmly now that, if your positioning is not right, don't even bother to pick up the phone. You should go back and re-explore the first half of this book and only go beyond this point when you are sure.

So, let's think about the effect we are likely to achieve if our inner voice tells us any of the following. 'I am not going to be able to get through. They are going to be too busy to talk to me. They are going to see me as a cold call. They are going to tell me they are very happy with their current arrangements. They are going to wonder who on earth I think I am. They are going to find holes in my logic. They are going to think I'm an idiot. I am not good enough. I don't know my product/service well enough. I will be wasting their time.'

And so on… well I guarantee that any success you get with that attitude will be purely accidental.

'The strongest factor for success is self-esteem. Believing you can do it, believing you deserve it, believing you will get it.' (Author unknown.)

Positioning incorporates self-esteem, belief, and the projection of that belief.

I find the technique of turning things on their head works well in many different situations. If you can't find the answer to what you do want, think of what you don't want, and reverse it. If we take that list of negatives and reverse them we get:

I am going to be able to get straight through. They are going to be available to talk. They are going to see me as a helpful consultant. They are going to feel they need me instead of, or more than, their current arrangements. They are going to recognise me as an expert. I am good enough. I know my product/service inside out. I will be solving a problem for them.

Now, I am not saying that simply willing a situation to change will actually change the outcome. What I am saying is that, when you are working on your approach with this positivity in mind, all that you translate will come out positively.

If you apply this positivity, and use a mind-set of being the expert who rang at the right time, solved an issue and created a new business relationship out of thin air… It will happen…

Maybe not every time, but it will. There's no hocus-pocus going on here, it's the way you are perceived that will create the success.

That perception is created by your positioning. You are the one who instigates the call, and you are the one who sets the tone. You are the one who is in control of what that person perceives.

So use the key questions I listed to adjust your positioning.

Who are you?

What gives you the right to disturb their day?

How can you change their life for the better?

Why should they want to hear from you?

What authority do you have that entitles you to advise them?

Further on in the book are some practical strategies, and writing your crib is an essential part of making successful calls. This correct positioning is vital if you are to write a great script, one that is full of confidence.

Again, it's this confidence that creates the attraction of your offering.

I regularly make proactive calls for my clients that end in the client thanking me for my call. That's due to the way that I position myself: as a helpful consultant; as someone who has changed their life for the better with my offering; and as someone who understands their needs and desires and has found a fit.

I have *not* positioned myself as a cold call or a nuisance.

If you are afraid to pick up the phone because you believe that the recipient will be annoyed that you rang, and you sound apologetic because of that fear, then you are setting the scene for a failed call.

You can tell immediately whether someone believes in what they are offering, because it all 'Translates' through their voice. As I mentioned in the 'T' of the toolbox, the belief behind the words makes a difference to the way in which those words are expressed and to the way in which they are perceived.

The number of telesales calls I receive in a single day that I could use as examples in this chapter is unbelievable.

One of the two main emotions that come across most frequently is nonchalance, which tells me that they don't believe or care what their offering is, that I am one of hundreds of people on a great list that they are working through, and that they don't care about the outcome either. As a result I do not trust them, believe them, or want to engage with them.

How do I recognise nonchalance?

It is translated through their voice, which is affected by their state of mind, their positioning (and belief), and the outcome they are expecting. All the elements of the toolbox.

The second emotion I get from cold callers is aggression. This tells me that they are expecting me to say no, that they are ready to fight me, that they are exasperated, which means they must be used to rejection, which in turn means no one else agrees to it, which means they must have a useless offering.

This, too, is translated through their voice, which is affected by their state of mind, their positioning (and belief), and the outcome they are expecting. All the elements of the toolbox.

One important factor that can strengthen your positioning is evidence.

This could be endorsements from clients and case histories – proof of the outcome when your offering has been applied.

Also, any accolades, awards and achievements that have been gained along the way, including surveys or opinion polls, will help. This evidence can also be used in the crib, which we will go through later in the book.

If your positioning is not right, then you must change the offering until it is. You can't turn a square peg into a round simply by saying 'It's round!' often enough. Go and find a round one!

Change Practice 4 – Ensure that you believe in what you are offering, then ensure that your positioning reflects that.

– Chapter 5 –

The foundations

Whatever you are using the phone for, whether it's building a community, raising awareness, selling or research, it is imperative that you have a good system which will diarise your calls, segment the status of each contact, and record your notes.

I strongly recommend a contact management system, but any form of database that can do these things will suffice.

It's important to have a firm structure in place so that you can prove your reliability and trustworthiness even before the relationship begins. Only last week I received four phone calls from the same salesman. The first time he contacted me to book onto my training course, then later he called me and left a message. When I returned the call, he confused me with somebody else, and started selling to me. Now I don't mind, I wasn't offended, but did I gain confidence in his sales ability? Did I feel that he was going to be reliable and trustworthy? The kind of person I wanted to buy from?

Maybe I would give him the benefit of the doubt this time.

Then I received a further call from him, returning the previous message that I had left… Getting confusing now, isn't it?

Now, I am the only Michelle Mills-Porter in the world (thank Heavens some might say!), and it's quite a memorable name. I can only conclude from this that he does not have a good working contact management system. If he did, he would only have to type in my name for all the details of our relationship to come up.

Every conversation we have should be précised on the notes section, so you are totally aware of the relationship, and of all the elements of that relationship.

In my opinion, your notes section is your biggest ally in building rapport.

Everyone wants to feel a bit special. Everyone wants to feel that you are interested in them. How are you going to achieve that if you don't make notes? Therefore a database that doesn't allow good notes to be made is not a system worth having.

Let's imagine I am contacting a potential donor for my charity. They have come up on my diary to remind me that I need to call them, and that they are likely to make a decision as to whether to sponsor an event I am holding.

'Hi, Anna, it's Michelle here from Cuddle Me, the charity that sends toys to orphans. Have I caught you at a good time?'

'Yes it's fine.'

'Great, thank you, I know you are busy so I'll be brief. Anna, we spoke back in May and you asked me to give you a bell back *around now* to talk about the *Autumn Fair*. You were organising an event yourself at the time. So I trust the *Sparkles Ball* was a huge success?'

The elements in italics are the things that I might have made a note of, and what I am drawing from for this whole conversation.

A sales call I made for a client recently included the following... 'So, Mike, you told me in *April* that you would want *evidence of the predicted margins* in order for you to add them to the presentation *at the board meeting next Wednesday*, so I've prepared a very snappy document which I'm e-mailing you right now, Do you want to have a quick look and see if it ticks your boxes while I'm here?'

And a while ago to a PA of a VIP... 'Hi Sharon, it's Michelle at Ethos. How's your week been?'

'Oh, I can't wait for the weekend, Michelle.'

'That good, eh? Never mind, only a couple of hours before you can crack open a *Chardonnay* and stick your feet in the *paddling pool* at home. You got anything planned with *Alice and Tom* while we've got the sun?'

The bits in italics were taken from my notes in my database. This is all just conversational information that has been noted that just helps me to remember who I am dealing with. If the relationship is important to me, then I will make the effort to learn about them, and I will help myself to remember by making notes.

You should log projection details; for instance, if it was a database of potential clients, then you would log what product they are interested in, when they are likely to be ready to buy, and at what price and quantity, and so on. The contact management system will be able to produce a good range of funky looking graphs, charts and pyramids, so that you can see your projections at a glance.

The diary is one of the most important aspects of a contact management system, and you should be accurate in your diary entries. People want to be contacted when they asked you to call them, not before and not after.

If a potential client asked you to call them next Wednesday, how do you think they would feel if you called them on Tuesday?

Most potential clients would feel that you hadn't listened, and that you see your own agenda as being more important than theirs.

When I ask this question in a workshop environment, it's amazing how judgmental we admit to being.

People say, 'I would think they are desperate', or, 'I would think they can't be trusted.' Or that they 'disrespect me!'

All very powerful reactions to something that might only have been an attempt to appear efficient.

What if you called them back on Thursday instead of Wednesday?

'I would feel that they can't be bothered, that I'm unimportant to them.' I've even heard, 'If I can't trust them to call back when they say they will, how can I trust them with anything?'

This is why a good contact management system is essential. If you have logged all this information then you can also forecast potential sales figures.

You can also forecast performance figures for the next quarter, the next year, thus avoiding peaks and troughs that can cause feast and famine in your business.

As long as you have this information, you will be able to predict when you might need to top up your activity, re-fill your pipeline, or even slot in a marketing campaign.

Client criteria

Do you know your client criteria?

It's really not good enough to say I want to work with 'Anyone who is… Anyone who needs… Any company that…' etc.

Understanding what you want, and who you want to do business with, can shape the entire direction of the company.

I remember standing back from my business one day, and realising that, because I had been fairly reactive in terms of my new clients, my company had started to gain a reputation for being attached to a certain sector.

The problem was, that wasn't necessarily the sector upon which I had wanted to focus.

When I decided to home in on the client criteria, it actually changed the direction of the business.

If you can identify who you want to work with it enables you to say 'No' to clients who are not going to add benefit to the brand of the organisation.

I suppose it's easy for me to apply this to my own business as I spent so long helping my clients to identify their client criteria when I was doing new business appointments. As I worked on a results basis, what the client wanted as new business opportunities had to be set in stone. We couldn't very well do all the hard work only to be told that the clients didn't want those opportunities.

I realised that it was a question many of my clients had never asked, and yet it is fundamentally important to identify it right at the start, so that the new business generation could grow in the right direction.

You can start off with the basics, in terms of turnover, sector, size, credit rating, number of employees, and then get even more specific, such as how may PCs they are using, the breakdowns of employee age, or their brand and reputation.

Having good client criteria can empower your positioning, strengthen your branding and allow you the freedom to steer your business in the right direction, rather than being led by what the market wants.

If you get enquiries from clients who do not fit your criteria, then set up an arrangement with another organisation you trust, so that you get an introduction fee, or have a reciprocal arrangement, so you don't lose out by passing on the business.

Source

How do you source your new business leads? How are you going to top up your pipeline? Are you a trawler fisherman, or are you an angler?

If you are a trawler, you will work with a higher number of less targeted organisations, because that is what works for your business. You may be an angler because you have tight criteria of who you want, or can work with.

I remember a time when I worked selling advertising space for business directories. We would work from pages ripped out of other directories, and just work top to bottom, calling every one.

Databases are usually not very well targeted, but that does depend upon how you sort the data. You should understand the basic criteria that needs to go to the top of the equation.

As an example, let's say that you want to source manufacturing companies in a particular city. You might choose to search all those within a 10 km radius. You only want those with a turnover of between £1 million and £10 million, and who have more than 50 employees. You only want head offices and limited companies.

That will give you a basic database to start work from, and you usually only pay for the number of companies you get in the list. However, it still pays to check through the list before you buy it, to allow you to sift out any that you don't think are accurate.

At the other end of the scale, you may only want to pick very specific organisations, and you might find these on open forums, or in social media groups.

LinkedIn is the very best social media platform for business at the moment. There are no signs of anything taking over either, and yet I still find people who don't use it.

You can find groups on LinkedIn that are populated by companies you might want to make contact with, and even identify the specific people you want to contact, including their direct telephone number and their employment history.

Cleansing

Whether you are using a database or handpicking your potential clients, it is important that you cleanse the data before you try to engage with them.

I had a great example from someone in my workshop just the other day, who said that he had witnessed a team of sales people that regularly went through the whole sales process, to only find out at the end that they were not relevant in some way. I think in this case their credit rating wasn't acceptable.

Why would you not check the credit ratings first, and then only contact the ones that you know are potential opportunities for you?

It might sound basic, but these fundamental rules are often overlooked, causing loss of time, effort and money to organisations large and small.

Just check through your database, and see if the new prospects are likely to need your service or product. This might be achieved through a little on-line research, or by a phone call. If you do contact them by phone, the strategy should be different from your introduction call. You are just checking details, so you can have a relaxed attitude about it.

The attitude should be that it doesn't matter if you get the information or not, it's not a life or death situation for you. This attitude is much less threatening than a sales call to some people on the other end of the phone. Quite often receptionists are taught to fear sales calls, or people trying to sneak their way through, so, if you use a light-hearted tone, and are friendly, there is no reason why they wouldn't help you get the information that you require.

Intelligence

This is the next step along from cleansing, and again, if you are using the phone for this, it should be a separate call from your main introduction. The intelligence process is for identifying the decision maker, and that is not always obvious from someone's title.

Every organisation has its differences, and it may be that, whilst the financial director might make the decision about your product or service in one organisation, it could be the managing director, or the marketing director in another. Identifying exactly who the right person is will save you from being knocked back by someone who isn't going to make the final decision anyway. It will be very difficult for you to speak to the managing director once the financial director has told you that they won't be interested, as it could seem as though you are undermining their authority, or just ignoring what they have said.

As rapport-building is vitally important in these relationships, it's easier to get it right the first time by ensuring that your intelligence is accurate.

In smaller organisations the relationships are often more intimate, and the person answering the phone may well be very close to, or even related to, the person you are trying to contact. Such people can often give you very accurate intelligence, as they are closer to the operations because they are in a smaller environment.

In a larger organisation you will find more departmental secretaries, support staff and personal assistants, so you will need to understand the infrastructure. Remember that these people are pivotal in whether or not you can reach the decision maker, therefore the relationship you have with them is of paramount importance.

There are many PAs who have been responsible for me getting to, and doing business with, VIPs, and there have been some who have been responsible for ensuring that I don't reach them.

However, there is no room for anyone who trains people in how to 'Get past the gatekeeper!' using tricks and lies. In my opinion, that's unforgivable. Always build rapport, always use good manners, and show your appreciation. It will get you much further than making an enemy of them will.

My sister was operations director in my previous company. Unfortunately, it was not uncommon for her to ring me with someone she was about to put through to me who had either told her a lie in order to reach me, or who had been rude.

Guess how much chance that person had of doing business with me?

You should gather direct phone numbers, full names and spellings of the decision maker and their PAs or secretaries, with correct titles and e-mail addresses.

If it helps, draw a picture of the structure and relay that in notes onto the database. This really helped me recently when I was dealing with a very large pharmaceutical company. There were several offices, and the person I needed was often in a different location, so it was important for me to know who was positioned where.

If I was told, 'He's in London today, let me put you through to that office', I would know from my detailed notes that his PA in London was Sarah. She would answer the phone with the office she was in rather than her name, but when I said, 'Oh, hi Sarah, it's Michelle here at Ethos', there was a much warmer basis to our conversation.

Intelligence calls should be made separately to your introduction/presentation calls and they are vital. Once armed with the intelligence, your call is no longer a cold call, but a tepid one at least! You won't appear to be a 'cold call' or a 'sales call' because you have done your research, and that can make all the difference as to whether you get through or not. If you ask for the details of the person you want to talk with and then ask to be put through in the same breath, you will fall likely into the category of sales call and be fielded away. I find that I happen upon many opportunities at this stage of my call, and sometimes make a sale, or get an appointment almost by accident and I am convinced that it is partly due to the fact that you are information gathering which comes with a relaxed attitude. My life doesn't depend on it, if you give me the information great, if not, that's OK too.

Whereas a 'sales' call often comes with a bit more tension, maybe some nervousness – the outcome is much more important – this tension can be translated and can cause distrust.

Pipeline

Keeping your pipeline topped up and clean is essential to any new business goal setting or targets.

In order for a pipeline to be effective, you should have clear categories and timings. For instance, if you set your database up to capture information about what the client is likely to be interested in, how often and when, then you will be able to forecast much more accurately.

You could categorise records in terms of their position in the buying cycle, such as hot prospects, warm or cold. You will be able to see the areas of the business that need more work, and you can set the calls into the diary system so that it reminds you when to call them.

I once sat next to an account manager who was trying to get into a massive organisation which had a roster of agencies that they only reviewed once every seven years.

Because he hadn't kept an accurate diary, he missed the opportunity to put his organisation forward at the right time. He missed the opportunity and would not get another chance for seven years!

Keeping your pipeline flowing is essential to avoiding those peaks and troughs that cause feast and famine, as mentioned earlier. There should always be the correct balance of people who are 'hot' (as in ready-to-buy, sign up, convert, or whatever your objective may be), warm and cold, and whatever other categories you choose. In this way, you will avoid stagnation in any area.

It's usually more rewarding to talk with people that you have built a relationship with and are ready to convert, but you must always ensure that you are starting new relationships, and moving warms forward at all times. In my experience, you need more colds than you do warms, and more warms than you do hots, as some will fall out the further up the scale the relationship is developed.

If you do not move a potential client forward or backward there is a danger that your pipeline may get blocked in the middle, and there is nothing more draining than opening up your database to see that you have a hundred calls to make that day! Where do you begin? It's a mammoth task, and it's too much. Therefore you should keep your database manageable, and flowing.

Don't be afraid to let an opportunity go if it's not going to convert. You can pick it up at a later date. Don't try to keep in touch once a week or once a month just for the sake of it; that is what will cause the blockages in your pipeline.

Momentum

There's a phrase I use to remind people of this subject.

'Use your ten pence!'

This dates me! Ten pence used to be the cost for the connection of a phone call, which would then last you for three minutes. After that, there would be a further charge.

Walking around my office I often heard my account managers failing to reach the person they wanted, and then simply saying they would call back and ending the phone call.

From a business aspect, I was paying 'ten pence' for every one of those calls, regardless of whether the account manager was having a three-minute conversation or a ten-second one.

If every account manager was doing the same thing, then there were going to be a lot of pennies wasted, per hour, per day, per week, month, year... That's a significant sum of money.

More than the financial aspect, I wanted to train my account managers to reach their contacts more effectively, and the 'ten pence' scenario worked for that, too.

When someone you are trying to reach is not available, I realised that, whereas I would find out whether they were out at a meeting or had just popped into another office, and when they would be back, and so on, some of my account managers were not doing that. They were just taking a chance, over and over again.

This might sound like an extreme example, but it is all too common. There is a senior sales person in the office where I am coaching at the moment, and she does this *all* the time. She just takes a shot, trying the contact and when she is told they are not in, she says, 'I'll call back another time.' The result is that she will be always treading water, not gaining momentum. It turns the process into a game of chance!

The cold hard fact is seen on that client's database: some of these accounts have been on the database for years, and they have *never* reached the decision maker, they just keep rolling the calls over and over again. I don't want to keep on about the financial implications here, but if you can imagine how much it has cost over the years to keep calling just a handful of accounts like that, it's like throwing money away.

So the subject was added to the training portfolio for those who tended to take a chance, rather than 'using their ten pence up'. Those account managers started to identify the best time to call, to understand their clients' movement patterns, and to calculate when they would be most likely to reach them.

On a large scale, this had a big impact. Whereas some people had previously been 'rolling over' their daily calls to the following day because that person wasn't there when they chanced to call, now they were homing in on the best time to try to reach that person.

Then they might set an alarm, so their database would remind them when the time was right, and they were catching their contacts much more often.

Just as an example: if someone is 'Not available at the moment', that could mean anything from 'She is not interested in talking to you', 'She is away from her desk', 'She's on holiday', 'Out at a meeting', 'In the middle of a report', or 'Powdering her nose!'.

If we don't know which of those it is, how can we know when to call her back?

Gently asking for clarification is completely acceptable. 'Oh, that's OK, is she out for the day, or will she be available in a while?' is enough to prompt more information to work with.

As long as every call you make is moved forward in some way, it was worth making.

The biggest drain on my company at the time was the ineffectiveness the lack of momentum created. If every account manager was spending an hour each per day making useless calls, then you can see the impact that would have on the company as a whole.

When you are making your contact calls, just check whether you are creating momentum. Did you move it forward in some way, even if it was just to establish a time when you are likely to reach them? Or collecting a direct line number?

It may be that the relationship is moved on to a closure or a 'blow out', as I call it in a sales environment. That's OK, because at least you are free-ing up your time to call someone else in their place.

Don't be afraid to let go of contacts, and to ask them directly if they would rather you didn't call back. It's pointless just treading water when you could be using your time more effectively somewhere else. Of course, the way you ask will determine whether or not you have a potential future relationship.

It's asking these questions that take you into the Genius level of communication, picking up on the hesitation that a person makes, or a change in their tonality. Then, if you pre-empt their response with a direct but well-positioned suggestion, it shows a great level of emotional intelligence, and it's a clincher for building rapport.

– Chapter 6 –

How to build rapport

Building rapport over the phone has to be achieved in seconds rather than in the minutes you might have in a face-to-face situation. We make up our minds whether we want to engage with someone instantaneously when we are using the phone.

It's important to be able to build rapport with everyone, and to treat everyone with respect, because they could be key in helping you to reach the person you eventually want to engage with.

We will go on to building rapport in a longer conversation with that target person in a moment, but first, I want to help with building rapport instantaneously with a receptionist or a secretary.

Opening phrases

One of the ways you can make an impression and be treated differently to all the other people who might call that day is to make yourself unique with an unusual opening phrase.

If a receptionist answers the phone in a particularly bright and pleasant way, I might comment on that immediately. So rather than going through the usual script such as: 'Hello, my name is Michelle and I'm calling from…' I might say 'Gosh, you sound happy! Can I come and work there?' or 'What a lovely way to answer the phone!' The probable response is that they will engage with you immediately! I've had everything from, 'Oh thank you, I do try' to 'It's all a big lie, I'm miserable really!'

Either way, you are engaging, and they will be far more likely to want to help you. You are making the effort and it will probably be reciprocated. You are not likely to get a negative response because we don't work like that as human beings. I find myself constantly reminding people that they are in charge of the relationship. If you start it, then you set the scene.

When people tell me they have had a bad day, that everybody is being rude, or nobody they talk with is interested, I believe they should take some responsibility for how they started the process.

I was doing some one-on-one coaching with a student the other day, and I noticed that her first line to client 1 was completely different to the one to client 2. When I asked why that was, she said that it was because client 1 had been short last time she called, and she was expecting the same response. Therefore she was being defensive right from the start.

We can go back to the Phone Genius toolbox here and think about positioning. But, I explained, that relationship is unlikely to become a warm one if she doesn't decide to engage differently, to start the process off in a more positive way.

As we discussed this further, she told me that she has some really warm, friendly relationships with some of her suppliers… and then it dawned on her that these suppliers were doing the same thing with her. They had instigated the relationship in a warm, friendly way, and she had reciprocated. Lesson learned!

Whatever your opening phrases may be, they should reflect your personality and should feel authentic to you. It doesn't need to be cheesy, gushy or salesy, just natural, like any conversation you might have with someone you already know.

I'm known for my chutzpah, so I have used, 'Oh dear, you don't sound very happy', showing empathy, and certainly not what you would expect from someone trying to sell something. Or when people have answered with, 'Good afternoon' when it should be morning, 'Are you wishing the day away too, then?'

Unexpected responses

This is just a way of showing your personality from the outset, and also giving you differentiation from all the other calls that day. When I have engaged with that person, and they have reciprocated and asked me how I am, I often respond with something unusual. I often use 'Bostin' thank you!' It's a colloquialism from the Black Country that means fabulous, or great. But those who are not familiar with the phrase will inevitably ask what on earth that means, and all of a sudden, you have a conversation going, rather than just going through the expected and boring introduction.

Really, anything apart from the standard, 'Fine, thank you, and you?' will tick my box. Anything that creates a conversation will work.

Also, when you are thanking people for their help, say something that they might not be used to, or compliment them. 'Oh, you are a star!' or 'I really appreciate your help, it makes a big difference.' 'You are really efficient, thank you.' These things are memorable!

Making notes

If you are speaking with someone who you might build a relationship with, for instance, a secretary or PA to the person you want to reach, then the most important thing you can do is remember some personal things about them. There is nothing more flattering than someone who seems to have an interest in you.

These people are usually an essential key to helping you reach the person you want, and I have several examples of someone in this position being the *only* reason that I ever reached the decision maker.

As I mentioned in Chapter 5, if you have a good contact management database this is easy, because you can make reams of notes. If you pick up on where people holiday, their kids' names, what wine they drink… it all helps.

When making my notes I include the conversation, along with the details. So long as the intention is good, this is not disingenuous. It's just being genuinely interested in the people I talk with.

During a follow-up chat with one PA, she told me that she had to leave early today, so I should try the VIP tomorrow, when she might be able to get me through. 'Oh, doing anything nice?' I said conversationally.

'No such luck, Michelle,' she said. 'My boy's not feeling well, and I have to fetch him from school.'

'Oh, no, poor Ben… Do you know what it is?'

Just my remembering her son's name really enhanced our relationship, and I would not have remembered unless I had made a note.

Of course, you need to apply common sense and emotional intelligence. After all, you are hoping to improve your conversations, not get arrested for stalking!

Mirroring

Mirroring is really important in building rapport on a subconscious level. I'm talking about mirroring volume, speed and language.

As a demonstration, imagine that friend you have who talks really loudly all the time, the one that people see coming and dive out of the way before they get captured? That's because the volume and the speed at which we speak is one of the best ways to break or build rapport.

You may notice that people who are really good communicators automatically do this, but when you are conversing with someone who talks loudly, you should increase your volume. Equally, if someone talks very quickly, you should speed up your delivery if you want to continue to stay in good rapport. If your contact talks very slowly and you naturally speak very quickly, you may initially be considered as over enthusiastic, or even desperate.

We are quite harsh in our judgements of others, more so over the phone than face to face.

VAKOG – The home base of language

Those of you who are familiar with neurolinguistic programming will know about VAKOG, a model that supposedly explains how the human mind stores and processes information using our five senses. Richard Bandler and John Grinder were the creators of neurolinguistic programming, and it was Peter Thomson, the platform speaker and trainer, who first showed me how it can help to build rapport on a subconscious level.

He called it 'the home base of language', and my interpretation of it is included in my training today. We can identify the way someone stores and processes information by listening to the words that they choose to use. If we can match that, then we can build rapport on a subconscious level.

It's really very simple although it might sound complicated.

> V – Stands for Visual (sight, imagery)
>
> A – Stands for Auditory (sound, speech)
>
> K – Stands for Kinaesthetic (sense, feeling, touch or movement)
>
> O – Stands for Olfactory (anything to do with smell)
>
> G – Stands for Gustatory (digestive, taste)

The first three are the most commonly used, and, if we can hear which words somebody is using, we can identify their chosen home base of language. Then, simply by using the same home base of language, we can build rapport on a subconscious level.

It's simple to identify with a short exercise.

Imagine you have won a competition to make over your home. You are choosing a suite of furniture for your lounge, and, of course, cost is no issue.

If you describe in single words or short sentences why you chose that suite of furniture, you should be able to identify your preferred home base of language, and therefore the way in which you store and process information in your mind.

So if the words you chose were, 'Style, it looks beautiful, or the ideal colour', then you would be using the Visual home base.

If you said that your suite of furniture was, 'Comfortable, soft, with wide seats', then it would be the Kinaesthetic.

The way you can pick this up in conversation is as follows:

I see what you mean – Visual
That sounds like a plan – Auditory
Let's do something together – Kinaesthetic
Show me the figures – Visual
Let me digest that and come back to you – Gustatory
Let's see how that feels – Kinaesthetic
I smell a rat – Olfactory
That chimes with me – Auditory

Although this example is very basic, it should give you the idea. If you can match someone's home base of language by using words that they would choose, you can build rapport with them on a subconscious level.

This is something you can pick up on immediately once you have practised it, and so it can easily be applied on the phone.

– Chapter 7 –

How to reduce the fear of rejection

We only fear the unknown.

There are many of us who put off our calls because we fear rejection. Even I can get a little nervous when I am working on a new project, so here are some tips on how to reduce that fear.

Use your homework

If you have prepared the foundations correctly, then you will already have identified your potential customers. Having done that, you can be more confident that they will have a need or a desire for your product or service, and that they are likely to be interested in what you have to say.

If you have cleansed the data, and made separate intelligence calls, then you have all the information you need to be able to make your call sound like a warm one, even if it is a cold one: you know who the right contact is, and you know their name, and maybe even their PA's name, and so on.

This will all give you more confidence, and so reduce the fear of rejection.

List and learn objections and your answers

If you know all the likely objections you will come across, and how you plan to answer them in a considered manner, then you will not fear rejection so much. After all, you can only fear the unknown.

So, list and learn all the reasons people might say 'no' to you, and remember the best way to reply to that 'no'. Once you have gone through all the 'noes' you can think of, ask a colleague or a peer for their opinion.

You can give them the scenario, and ask why they might say 'no'. Once you have worked on all those, I say ask a child! They can come up with some great reasons to say 'no' that you may not have thought of.

Once you have them all, your fear of rejection will be reduced.

I'm referring to your introduction here, so you haven't got an existing relationship yet.

If you understand that it is the client's choice, and that they have the right to say 'no', it can also help to reduce the fear of rejection.

It's not usually personal, especially if it's a cold call. Ask yourself why they are saying 'no', and respect their decision.

Later in the book we will go through understanding what an objection is, and what it is not, and I am not suggesting that you shouldn't try to overcome objections. Rather that it's not likely to be about you. It's not that they don't like you, or that they don't like your offering. It's much more likely, in a phone scenario, that the time is not right, or that they are distracted. They might be up against a deadline, or have a crisis in their organisation.

You can always ask if you can call back another time rather than never calling them again.

As I've mentioned previously, the brain is designed to spot patterns. To quote top executive coach, Pete Freeman:

> We are constantly looking for connections and latch on to exceptions or the unexpected more than anything else. If we receive feedback we ignore the nine positive comments and focus on the one negative. In the same way, we naturally tend to fret if someone doesn't return our message or if they don't seem to warm to us.
>
> There are two points to make here:
>
> Firstly, if someone doesn't respond, then it is almost certainly circumstance rather than something personal. After all, we are all too busy most of the time these days.
>
> Secondly, everyone understands the world through the lens of their own assumptions and past experiences. If they haven't warmed to you, its more likely to be because you sound just like their 'ex', or they had just had some bad news when they first met you. It could be anything!

If you fret about these kind of things, which you clearly can't control, and if you worry about being universally liked by everyone then you'll waste a lot of time and energy getting nowhere. Trust in your own personality, and focus on the people who do like you and with whom you want to work.

There is more on finding the right time to engage in Chapter 9, *How to engage with the contact.*

STOP
Remember the toolbox?
    State of mind
    Translation
    Outcome
    Positioning
Check this before you pick up the phone, and you will reduce the fear of rejection.

– Chapter 8 –

How to make a cold call sound like a warm call

'Do you believe that phones are on the way out?' is a question that I get asked all the time. My answer to this question is no, I don't. Truth be told, I have asked myself that question for the last 15 years, and although telephones will continue to evolve, I believe they will still be a communication tool for many years to come.

Another question I am asked frequently is why even the gentlest of cold calls is treated with negativity, even if it is just to find out what a company does. The problem here is based around our description of a cold call. Research and intelligence calls should be separate calls to the introduction, which is the 'cold call'. My rule is that when you have a new contact to reach, you should first perform an intelligence call. This is to establish that they are the correct person, with the correct authority. You can also find out the spelling of their name, their e-mail address, their direct line and their PA's details. This call should be made to the receptionist, the PA, or even someone else in the same department. The introduction call is then made to the contact separately.

If you do this then your intelligence calls can be made with a completely different mind-set and attitude. You are just checking information, so you are not likely to be greeted with defence or scepticism. You are not going to try and get through to someone, or try to sell to someone.

Subsequently, your 'cold call' will immediately sound like a warm call, because you are armed with the information you need. If you sound like a cold call, you will be rejected or dismissed. You are likely to feel rejected, and hate your job. Who wants that?!!

So the first rule is, sound like a warm call.

Let's look at what a cold call at reception might sound like.

'Good morning, my name is Michelle Mills-Porter, calling from a company called Ethos Development Ltd. I need to speak with the person responsible for grounds maintenance, could you tell me who that is and put me through please?'

Do you think that sounded right? Is it polite? Does it sound like a cold call?

Let's take that paragraph apart.

I'm going to have to ask you to use your imagination here, as a lot of this will be in the way the words are delivered.

I want you to imagine that I delivered this quite quickly and in a fairly monotonous voice.

This would suggest that my attitude is bored (monotone). It may have sounded like the millionth phone call I had made that day.

I start off giving my full name – a formal introduction suggesting that they don't know me. I also use the full company name, which clearly indicates that no one there knows of my company, therefore there can be no existing relationship.

I don't know who I need to speak to, I've not bothered to do any homework. There's no rapport, nor warmth, in this paragraph, is there? I may have just done enough to appear courteous.

This stinks like a cold call and it will get treated like one!

So let's imagine what a warm call might sound like:

'Hi, it's Michelle here at Ethos. I need to quickly speak with Liz, Liz Windsor about her grounds maintenance. Could you please pop me straight through?'

This time, please imagine that my tone is confident and bright.

I have abbreviated my name, thus suggesting familiarity. I have also abbreviated my company name, which suggests they should know my company, too.

I have also suggested that it's just a quick call, so it wouldn't really hurt if they were to put me through. It takes the heat away from double checking who I am, and from finding out whether it's a relevant issue, in the same way as it does when I explain why I am calling, '… about her grounds maintenance.'

This also suggests that I am used to their in-house system.

At reception they might have been briefed to ask who it is calling, who they want, and what it's about… The fact that all receptionists are briefed in the same way doesn't make any difference. If they feel that I am used to their system, then it stands to reason I must have been through it before. Again, this implies there is an existing relationship. (See below the rules about truth.)

The final sentence is incredibly powerful. 'Could you please pop me straight through.'

Some people who have studied neurolinguistic programming might tell you that this is an embedded command. Others say it is not, but it is a directing question. The truth is that I haven't deliberately followed any strategy with this, it's just the way in which I get more positive responses. It's born from instinct, emotional intelligence, and testing!

I know that if I place the 'please' at the beginning of the sentence it rips out the strength of that sentence. It does the same thing when I place the 'please' at the end. It turns a powerful, confident sentence into a submissive one.

Let's face it, although I am being polite in my request, it's not really a request. I am expecting to get through, and here's one of those strange things; when you are confident about what you want, people often comply.

Now, I said that there are rules regarding being truthful, so don't forget the two keys are authenticity and personality. So if the receptionist asks you, 'Is she expecting your call?' don't fudge it, be truthful. (But inject some personality!)

If you are asked, 'Have you spoken with her before?' Then again, be truthful.

The way I often handle it is with humour and chutzpah. If asked, 'Is she expecting your call' I might say, 'Not unless she has a crystal ball!' then go into explaining why I am calling without delivering the entire pitch to someone who probably doesn't really want to know. They are just being diligent. Depending upon what I pick up from the person I am speaking to, I might not use so much chutzpah. I might just say, 'Sorry, no, I always sound a bit over-familiar,' and then explain a bit more. After all, this question is about finding out a little more out before they put you through.

Talking chutzpah, I'll tell you about a couple of success stories that taught me a lot, using my chutzpah.

I didn't know what the word meant, but when several people had told me that they liked my chutzpah, I thought I would look it up.

It's of Yiddish origin, and apparently in current terms, it means courage, audacity or mettle. (Pronounced Hutz-spa! With a lovely throaty noise that you just can't translate with words!) I believe there were more negative connotations attached originally, but it was always meant in a cheeky sense when delivered to me.

Chutzpah – Goes a long way!

There was a potential client who was very interested in completing some business with me. We had built a really nice relationship over the phone and I was just waiting for confirmation to go ahead with the order, when he went very quiet on me. I didn't seem to be able to get a response, and then it felt as if he was avoiding my calls.

I rang in one morning and spoke with the receptionist, Liz, who was as bright and cheerful as ever when I announced myself and asked if my contact was in.

'Oh hi, Michelle, yes, let me just put you through…'

A few moments later, she came back on the phone.

'Erm… I'm sorry Michelle. He, erm… appears to be out of the office. Can I pass a message on for you?'

Liz had already said that he was in the office, and was now obviously struggling with telling me that he didn't want to take my call. So I made my excuses, and said I would call back.

So, what makes someone want to avoid you, when you have done everything right and built great rapport? It really puzzled me.

I knew we had an informal, fun relationship, so I decided to do something completely different. I went through my client notes and found one that said he had a particularly soft spot for the singer, Kylie Minogue. I rang back later and in a demure voice I asked to speak with my contact, without introducing myself.

'Can I ask who is calling please?' said Liz.

'Yes it's Kylie.' I said with confidence.

Liz continued, 'Kylie…?' urging me to give her more information.

'Kylie Minogue', I said firmly and confidently.

It sounded as if Liz wanted to laugh, but how did she know that I wasn't a very important potential client with the same name as the pop star? So she kept up her professionalism, 'Err, I'll just try and get you through. Bear with me…'

The next thing I heard on the line was a very sheepish man's voice… 'Errr, Hello?'

'John!' I exclaimed! 'Why would you pick up the phone to Kylie Minogue and not me?!'

Well, he'd been well and truly caught out, so what could he do but laugh about it? I told him that I didn't mind what the news was, just so long as he *talked* to me. It was then that he told me he had lost his budget to another department in the organisation. I realised that, if you have built a particularly good relationship with a potential client, it is sometimes hard for them to let you down, and that is why they might not call you back.

So what's the worst that can happen?

We survived that episode, and when he got his budget back we did some work together. Me being authentic enhanced the relationship.

So the important point is that I am *not* asking you to be someone you are not, nor am I coaching you in pretending to be famous people in order to reach a contact. What I am saying is, you should be as comfortable on the phone as you are face to face, and allow your personality to show through. This is my sense of humour, and I knew I had a good relationship with this contact.

All too often as soon as the phone is raised to our ears, we put on a phone voice, or think that we have to be ultra-professional, when really what is required for building rapport is to allow our own personalities to shine through.

The second lesson here is that, if someone is not returning your calls, and you know that you have a good relationship, it might mean that you have built such a good relationship with them that they don't want to let you down. So it may be that they cannot now move ahead, or that their budgets have been moved, or that they have decided to use another supplier but don't want you to feel bad.

I have found time and time again that the best thing to do if someone is not returning my calls is to let them off. Pre-empt what the reason might be, so you could leave a message on their voicemail that goes like this: 'I realise that you might not want to go ahead right now, but it would be useful to have a chat just so I can close off the record on my database.' Or, 'I'm thinking that you may have changed your mind, and that's fine, but perhaps we can just have a brief chat so I can make some notes for the future.'

It's taken the pressure off them, so they might find it easier to call you back if they had decided against your proposal. If they had just been very busy, it may be enough to prompt them to call you anyway.

I am often asked, 'How far can you go over the phone?' and I suppose the real question there is, again, 'Why are we putting on airs and graces?' The way we speak face to face is the way we should speak over the phone, and you can build just as solid a relationship if you can learn to master this.

It's very important that we don't try to be something we are not. Human beings can sense authenticity, and they can sense falseness. It may just be an uneasy feeling, or a lack of connection, but it will be sensed – and, guess what? It will be sensed over the phone, too!

However, there has to be a limit in terms of how far you can go.

I'm going to share with you now a very valuable lesson about how far is too far. And I sincerely hope you learn from this.

It was in the early days of my company, and I was working with a small marketing agency who gave me a massively impressive target list with which to try to set appointments. I have since learned that, if I'm going to spend my time breaking down the doors of some of the top names in the world, I should save them for the most deserving clients, but at the time I wanted to prove my worth. One of their targets was Microsoft.

They were adamant that they wanted an appointment with the marketing director responsible for the marketing agency roster, so I set about my approach.

We'll skip forward to where I had established and built a great relationship with his PA, 'Karen'. She had all the details about why I wanted to reach 'Michael' and he had agreed in principle to talk with me, so it was now just a question of trying to pin him down. He was notoriously difficult to reach, as he was so busy.

I had learned so much about Karen's kids, her favourite wine and various other bits of information through our general conversations that we felt like friends when we spoke. On this particular day I had been advised to call Michael at lunchtime, as he was in a pretty intense meeting, but would break for lunch.

So I called at the exact time that Karen had suggested, only to find that the meeting was still in progress.

Karen suggested I tried in ten minutes, which of course I did.

No, the meeting had still not broken for lunch, 'Try in another ten minutes.'

Ten minutes later, I rang Karen to find out that they had asked for lunch to be taken into the meeting room, as they were working through.

A quick reassessment of the situation suggested that I should continue to try to reach him today, as he was expecting my call, and I hadn't harassed him at all. It was his PA who had been taking my calls and advising me. By this time, though, she seemed to feel bad about not getting me through, and was as determined as I was to make that conversation happen.

'Michelle, call back towards the end of the day, I know he has to get a 4 o'clock train, it's very important, so he will definitely finish the meeting before then.'

I rang when she had suggested, at half past three, to find that they were just tying up the meeting.

Things were getting exciting now, and the tension was building. I wouldn't have long, but I was actually going to pin him down and get my chance to explain why Microsoft should be interested in meeting with a little insignificant marketing agency… (!) OK, we'll cross that bridge when we get to it!

Five minutes went by, and in my excited state I rang on Karen's direct line.

'Hello?' said Karen.

'Karen, it's Michelle, is he free?' I asked excitedly.

'Five minutes more, Michelle,' she said. 'He's just finishing. Don't worry I will get you through!'

Now things were getting tense, and even though I needed the loo, I wasn't going anywhere.

Precisely five minutes later, I pressed redial…

'Karen – Michelle!' I stated.

'Oooooh, Michelle! I'm so sorry!' she said. 'He rushed straight out and went straight for his train, he said he couldn't miss it! I am *so sorry*!'

'Oh, no!' I couldn't believe it. 'Never mind, give me his mobile…!'

And she did!

What? She just gave me the mobile number of the marketing director at Microsoft! Well, I wasn't about to argue, so I thanked her and she wished me luck.

Although I wouldn't usually call a client on a mobile, he had given permission for me to call, and was expecting me to, and I had to strike while the iron was hot!

I rang the mobile number and a flash of insecurity swept over me. What if he doesn't appreciate that I have called him on his mobile? Suppose Karen gets into trouble for giving me the number?

But before I could talk myself out of it, it started to ring.

Then, half excitedly and half nervously, I tried to compose myself, and to think through what I was going to say.

It rang, three times, four times, then through to voicemail. 'Hi, you've reached Michael...' The tension was just impossible. Now I had to leave a voicemail message that would entice him to return my call, so it had to be exciting and high energy, but not sound as if I'm desperate. After all, he's left the office, therefore it's like after office hours!

I started to type in the database to make a note of the message I'd left for him, and as I did so, the date and time popped up. 14th February? That's Valentine's day! I hadn't realised it was Valentine's Day!

Just then, the message came to an end, and the beep sounded...

No time left, I had to leave a message, now!

'Happy Valentine's Day to you!' I was singing to the tune of 'Happy Birthday'. 'What on earth am I doing?' I thought frantically. 'Happy Valentine's Day, to you...!' I continued. Still in song, I finished, 'It's Michelle from ____ Marketing, please call me back.'

Oh, my life! What had I done? He was going to think I was mentally disturbed! He would be horrified at my level of unprofessionalism. He would make a formal complaint about me, my client was going to fire me for bringing their name into disrepute, what had I done?

Head in hands, I tried to think of a damage limitation plan. What could I do to save Karen's job, my reputation, and my client?

My phone rang.

'Hello?' I said sheepishly.

'My wife doesn't understand me!' came this pleading voice.

'Twenty years!' he continued, 'She *never* buys me so much as a card, here I am leaving work early to go and make her Valentine's Day a special one, take her to the best restaurant, and what thanks do I get?'

It was Michael.

'You've really made my day!' he said.

We ended up having such a laugh and he actually said to me, 'Michelle, if your agency has *half* the personality you do, then we can do business!' and he wasn't just talking about getting onto the roster, he was so impressed that, if the meeting with my director went well, he was going to give us a piece of work!

What a result!

I couldn't have got a hotter appointment for my client and I learned a very valuable lesson here. What's the worst that can happen?

Now, I am not encouraging you to put on an act or to do things that are outside your comfort zone. This happens to be who I am, and I was just natural.

I was with a client recently and we were sitting in a hotel having tea.

I chatted to the waitress as she brought our drinks, and I called her by name; we had a chuckle about something. My client asked me if I knew *everyone*?

'No, I don't know her,' I said.

'But you chatted to her like you were friends. And you called her by name.'

'Yes, she's wearing a name badge, why would you not?'

This is a funny experiment, actually. Maybe this is more relevant in the UK than some other countries, I don't know.

You know when someone in a shop serves you, and they are wearing a name badge? Well, if you don't already, try using their name when you say, 'Thank you.' Some people are really surprised, and look at you as if they are trying to recall where they know you from. That's just proof we are not doing it often enough.

Some others are openly chuffed that you have engaged with them, and reciprocate. As I said, maybe it's a trait of the UK that we don't use people's names as much as they do in other countries. I'll have to check that and look at the results.

Be natural over the phone, and you will build relationships, with those that you attract, and you will not with those you repel – just as you do in face-to-face situations.

– Chapter 9 –

How to engage with the contact

Please remember that, although I encourage natural communication above any technique, some etiquette is required when engaging on the phone. Many people seem to forget this.

Have you noticed how annoying it is when someone calls you, and just talks at you?

The general reaction is one of immediate suspicion. Maybe it's because that person has not had the manners to engage correctly, or because usually people stop them, and therefore they are desperate to get their message out.

Either way, it creates a negative reaction. My guess is that quite often people are taught incorrectly, and the fear is that someone can disengage with you more quickly on the phone. It's just a quick, 'No thank you', and the call is ended.

If you were to meet someone face to face, you wouldn't just flop out your 'pitch' as soon as being introduced, so it can't be done on the phone either.

It's worth remembering that the correct etiquette in any situation is to ask permission first.

This is just as simple as, 'Have I caught you at a good time?' or, 'Are you OK for a moment?' It doesn't have to be anything too formal.

Now, some old-fashioned cold-calling trainers might be busting a blood vessel right now, because if you were ever privy to any sales techniques of old, you would have heard that you NEVER ask an open-ended question!

What that means is that you are meant to cajole the other party into saying 'Yes' all the time, and not allow them to 'get away.' So by only asking closed-ended questions, the one to which the contact can only really give you the answer you want, you keep 'control' of the conversation.

An open-ended question might be something like, 'So how do you see the company developing?' In contrast with a closed-ended question, which would be something like, 'So are you positive about the company's development?'

Quite frankly, you have to be supersensitive when conversing on the phone, and I avoid such concrete sales techniques because anyone who has been on a sales course will recognise it as a sales technique.

Who likes feeling manipulated, or being sold to? I don't. When I ask people in a workshop how they feel if they realise that the person they are having a conversation with is using a sales technique on them, the response is usually a very harsh one. People find it abhorrent.

Therefore by asking someone's permission to talk, you are also taking yourself outside the expected sales scenario. If you are asking questions that a sales person would not ask, then perhaps you are not a sales person.

I'm using 'sales' as the example here more for reference than anything else. Usually, when we are reaching out to someone using the phone, we have an end game in mind, so in a sense we are 'selling' ourselves, even if we only want someone to join our cause or our mailing list, or to give us their opinion.

So please bear with me using that example.

Once you have asked their permission, a bit of appreciation can go a long way.

'Thank you, Sam, I realise how busy you are, and I appreciate that.'

Or, 'Thank you Sam, I'll keep it brief, I know you are busy.'

Respect their position, their valuable time, and their attention.

Finally – ask if they want to play

What do I mean by that?

Well, I mean we are again keeping a mutually respectful, mutually positioned conversation balanced here. I wouldn't want to talk with someone who was under duress, or who would rather not be talking to me, so I'm just checking that we are on the same page.

A simple question such as, 'Is this something you are interested in?' or 'Is this a subject of concern for you?' is sufficient to check their level of engagement.

My advice here is if they are not ready to engage further, then you need to take a step back, and either try to re-establish a level of interest, or find out if there is a reason they are not engaged. Maybe they are not the right person, or maybe you have mistimed your call.

Either way, do not continue if they do not want to.

I use a simple visual reminder in my mind's eye of a golf ball circling a hole. You cannot tap it in until it has stopped moving and it is lined up. In the same way, you shouldn't try to 'close' a sale when all the client's objections haven't been answered, and you shouldn't try to make a proposal unless the client is on the same page as you.

– Chapter 10 –

The three stages of listening

This is one of those areas that can shoot you way ahead of the game. The old saying is that we were born with two ears and one mouth and we should use them in that proportion.

I've literally just finished a phone conversation with someone claiming to be fabulous on the phone, and wanting a position. She talked over me several times, finished my sentences twice and rambled on incessantly for most of the 15-minute conversation. Even if I make allowances for nervousness, I'm not sure that I will be recommending her to anyone I know at this stage.

Before that I had a 40-minute phone conversation with someone I know fairly well face to face. This was the first time we had had a long conversation on the phone, and if we had met in this way, I would probably not have developed the relationship.

That sounds a bit harsh, but it's a reminder of how quickly we judge others when we have that contraption stuck to our ear – far more quickly than we do in person.

I can't believe how much he rambled on! He digressed several times, and at one point I timed how long I was silent. We got into double figures.

We can't do this!

There is no way to tell whether the other person is still engaged unless you check. No one wants a one-way conversation! It's not a webinar, it's a conversation, it goes two ways.

I could have put the phone down, and walked away, and run a bath – and he would have been none the wiser for the best part of 15 minutes.

Therefore included in listening is *checking*.

(See active listening, the second stage, page 97.)

It was during a meeting with a lovely friend of mine, (Jude Jennison, who I mentioned earlier in the book on the subject of her Leadership with Horses training) that I learned how others describe the different stages of listening. Putting it together with what I had learned over the years really helped me to put it into easy categories, which enables me to coach others.

Waiting to speak

Waiting to speak is the first stage of listening, and we are all guilty of it sometimes.

It was Peter Thomson who first suggested that this is why we rarely remember a joke, because when we are being told a joke we are so concerned with thinking of one to reply with that we rarely take in what is being said to us effectively. 'Oh, oh I know one!'

If you catch yourself doing this, then stop it! It's very annoying. It's not very complimentary to the other person.

You can tell when someone is doing it with you while conversing on the phone when you hear the 'Yeah, yeah' noises, or 'Hmm, hmm', almost hurrying you along to finish your sentence. Those who are used to communicating on the phone will know instinctively when someone is not fully engaged, but if you are not, you might have to listen out for these giveaways.

You might hear raised excitability in their voice because they want to tell you something, or because they want to challenge you with an experience they have had that contradicts what you are saying.

If you pick up that someone is in this stage of listening, then you should let them speak and not try and get to the end of your point. A simple, 'Sorry, go on…' or 'You were saying?' is enough to hand over the conversation until they have said what they want to.

It's this relaxed attitude that will make people think you are not pressurising them, and it takes you outside the 'selling' box in people's minds.

Active listening

The second stage of listening is active listening. It's a phrase that is bandied about by many, and truly understood by few.

In my opinion, active listening is not just ensuring that you are hearing what the client is actually saying, but also feeding it back to them, to check, as I mentioned in my rant at the start of this chapter.

If I think about what I do when I am making notes on an important conversation with someone I want to build rapport with, I make quite a few assumptions based on what the client is *not* saying. It's reading in between the lines. What I do with that information is feed it back to the client to ensure it's accurate.

As an example, I can assume that if someone tells me they only work until 3 p.m. every day they may have children, and have to collect them from school. It's not accurate until I feed it back and check, but it's being more proactive with your listening skills that can set you streets ahead of others.

Similarly, if someone hints that they are going to be partying heavily all weekend, then they might not be the family type with kids. Again, it's only an assumption until it is fed back and checked, so I might do this by asking questions that could give me a clearer indication.

After all, we all know it's not good to assume. 'It makes an ass out of you and me,' is the old saying that everyone seems to quote.

It was Jude who suggested I use a role play exercise in my workshops and it works really brilliantly. She used the example of talking about a favourite holiday.

One person talks about their holiday, while the other person listens. We're not feeding back at this time, we are just learning to listen in between the words. I talk about my holidays in the Maldives, and how I spend most of my time under the water, and how amazing the sea life is.

You might think it's not the ideal holiday destination for young children, especially with the complicated travel to get to the islands, so you might assume that I don't have young children. You might also assume that I am a wildlife lover, not a sunbather and either a diver or a snorkeler. Unless you feed back and check, you won't know, but it's a great place to start.

If I were to talk about my caravan holidays in Wales I might divulge some things that would make you assume I am a family-oriented person, or that I am quite spiritual. The fact that I avoid the main holiday season would tell you much more than that, too!

When you are feeding back to me and checking, it makes me feel valued and appreciated, which helps to build rapport, but there is more to it than that.

You also need to be listening for emotions, for feelings that are being imparted by the use of the voice, when they get excited about something, or when they are talking on a subject that really touches them.

A person's values is another key area to being able to build rapport with them, and you can pick those up using your intuition in the words they use, coupled with the tone of their voice. If, when talking about my holiday, I mention freedom, the open space, or being in nature, these words will give you signs about my values. If I describe being around the family, or a night out with friends, this also tells you about my values and my preferences.

You should be able to learn little bits about their behaviour type too. Are they easy going and laid back, or driven and direct?

There is a section of this book on behaviour profiles (Chapter 6), and you can't learn to understand people's behaviour profiles if you don't learn to actively listen. What you pick up by listening actively can be information about the way they like to communicate, and what's important to them, so, when it comes to the time to make your presentation, you will know exactly what is most likely to fit their wants and needs.

Environmental listening

The third stage of listening is environmental listening, and that, in short, is the ability to be able to pick up on what is happening around you, as well as in the immediate conversation.

When working on the phone, it means picking up on what is happening around your contact, and how that might affect their attention or their decision. I can't stress enough how important this part of the book is to being able to create that sense that you are almost psychic. If you can pre-empt the client's needs in advance, you will get ahead in leaps and bounds in your relationship building.

It's a tricky art to practise, because you risk concentrating on the background activity so much that you lose concentration on the conversation, so it's probably best to start in social environments. Networking meetings, or business gatherings are a great environment for this, so while you are having a conversation with someone, try to listen to what's going on in the background as well.

It's just as if you are in a busy restaurant talking with friends, but waiting for your order to be called out.

As an example of how this works on the phone, I once called a company just before the Christmas holidays, and as the phone was answered I could hear laughing in the background, and the chinking of glasses… The receptionist sounded in very high spirits when she answered the phone, and I immediately acknowledged the situation by saying, 'Oh! It sounds like fun over there!' Rather than just going straight into the corporate introduction.

'Yes', she said, 'we're breaking up this afternoon.'

Being mindful of that situation is simply more natural than ignoring it, and people respond in a friendlier manner.

'Oh, I see. Well I don't want to dampen the party spirits by talking shop, is everyone breaking up today?'

It may be that some people are not, and that the person I need to speak to is still working, but if they are not, it's probably not the best time to try to engage.

It may sound like an extreme, but imagine you call into a company and you can hear a fire alarm in the background, or lots of hustle and bustle. If you start the conversation taking that into consideration, you will be treated more favourably than if you just continue regardless.

'Sounds like I've called at an inconvenient time.'

'Oh, the fire alarm is stuck and we can't seem to stop it, it's getting so annoying!'

If your response is one of empathy, such as, 'Well, I'll leave you to sort that out, and perhaps try again this afternoon…' then you stand a good chance of the receptionist being grateful.

The key is that, when you call back later and make reference to your earlier call, you stand a much better chance of being treated with the same empathy that you showed.

'Oh, it sounds a bit calmer there now, I called earlier and you were in the middle of the fire alarm fiasco.'

'Oh, yes, it was a bit of a nightmare, but we've got it sorted now, thank you. Now, how can I help you?'

Once you are used to listening to the background activity as well as the conversation in hand, you might start to pick up on tension or a sense of urgency just by the way people are talking, or general noise in the background.

You should then progress on to being able to tell if someone is not fully engaged. For instance, if the line seems to become a little muffled, it may be that the person you are talking with has temporarily moved their receiver out of the way of their mouth, so they can mouth or whisper something to someone else. This might suggest that they are trying to do several things at once, or that they are needed quite urgently.

Some other things that you might hear are paperwork being rustled, the telling 'click' of someone putting you on mute in the middle of a sentence, or if their voice becomes slightly suppressed, it could be that they have their head buried in some paperwork while still talking with you.

In these situations it is better to try to pre-empt what the contact might want, and suggest another time for your conversation.

A direct revelation of what you believe may be happening won't be acceptable of course, but a gentle suggestion may bring a wave of relief to the contact.

'So, I don't want to bombard you with too much information, I can tell that you are busy. Suppose I call you back tomorrow at a time that suits you, and we can talk about it in more depth?'

Almost every time I have done this, the contact has thanked me for my insight and invited me to call them back. Of course, when I do call them back, I am now a much warmer call. I have been invited to call, they are expecting me, and they usually feel more obligated to give me their attention.

In many cases the contact has replied, 'No, I'm sorry, I was just a little distracted, please go on,' and it brings their attention back into focus.

Occasionally the contact has answered by saying that they don't think they are the person I should be speaking to.

In that case, it's a lesson in ensuring that you do your due diligence beforehand.

As Jude says, 'You've mastered the art of listening when you can listen at all three levels at the same time so you notice what your own thoughts are in response to what is said, you understand what is important to the person speaking and you are aware of the environment that you are in and how that informs you.'

– Chapter 11 –

Behaviour profiling over the phone

I subscribe to the Everything DiSC® profiling methods by Wiley. DiSC® is a behaviour assessment tool that I have used for more than a decade. I find it incredibly useful in helping me to quickly understand the reason for someone's behaviour (even in a very short space of time) and therefore how to best engage with them.

Wiley's solution-focused DiSC® products are used in thousands of organisations worldwide, including major government agencies and Fortune 500 companies. Every year, more than a million people worldwide participate in programmes that use a Wiley DiSC® assessment.

The DiSC® model began with an American psychologist called Dr William Moulton Marston. In 1928, he wrote a book called *The Emotions of Normal People* which laid the foundations for the modern day DiSC® model.

In addition to being a lawyer and a physiological psychologist, he also has two other claims to fame... Firstly, he was part of the team that developed the lie detector. Secondly, he was the inventor of the comic book character Wonder Woman. In 1956, Walter Clarke developed an assessment tool from Dr Moulton Maston's work and then John Greier contributed further in 1958.

I did my DiSC® training through the Academy of High Achievers, run by the wonderful Tony Burgess and Julie French. I've used DiSC® for years now and it is the easiest and clearest behaviour profiling system I have seen.

I will not suggest that you should make snap judgments on a person's behaviour profile, but just as VAKOG serves us in building rapport with people, so can a touch of DiSC®.

Tony and Julie taught me that there are two main considerations that suggest which behaviour profile is being displayed.

The first is whether the person you are speaking to is fast paced or slower paced. This is something you can easily tell over the phone by the ways in which someone speaks, and the urgency with which they ask for information, or handle the conversation.

This would suggest that, as shown in the diagram, they are displaying either 'D' or 'i' behaviour if they are faster paced, OR 'C' or 'S' behaviour if they are slower paced.

The second consideration is whether they are task oriented or people oriented. This can be picked up easily in conversation. Are they more concerned with facts and figures, or with how their team will respond, what their client might think, and so on.

If they are task oriented they will either be displaying 'D' or 'C' behaviour, and if they are people oriented, they will be displaying 'i' or 'S' behaviour.

Now of course we are all an amalgamation of all the behaviour types, but we usually find we have one or two prominent behaviour types, and that there is a pattern for every scenario.

D	i
Dominance	Influence
Fast Paced / Task Oriented	Fast Paced / People Oriented
1. Action Taker	1. Enthusiastic
2. Results Oriented	2. Likeable
3. Decisive	3. Cheerful
a. Aggressive	a. Undisciplined
b. Pushy	b. Disorganised
c. Rude	c. Over Personal
C	S
Conscientiousness	Steadiness
Slow Paced / Task Oriented	Slow Paced / People Oriented
1. Accurate	1. Supportive
2. Orderly	2. Dependable
3. Perfectionist	3. Calm
a. Judgmental	a. Indecisive
b. Critical	b. Wishy-Washy
c. Negative	c. Pleaser

The numbered descriptions in each category are the characteristics that you may well pick up during a conversation. The three lettered descriptions in each category are how people of other behaviour profiles may see them. There is no right or wrong, it's just different. If we can understand which behaviour pattern someone is displaying, then we can build rapport by matching our language, and also by understanding what their requirements are, what motivates them, and what will not be of interest to them.

For instance, if we classify the person we are speaking to as fast paced, and interested mainly in the numbers, then we need to deliver that aspect of the conversation. If we start talking about the benefits to the employees within the business, that's not going to be as important to them, and they might switch off.

Equally, if we are talking with someone who is slower paced and more considered in their decision making, and who skates over the numbers, but is more interested in how your offering can benefit their clients, then there is little point in trying to win them over by talking about financial savings or profitability.

This is a fascinating subject, and I am certainly not doing it justice by simplifying it in this way. However, since we have such a short space of time on the phone, I have found this abbreviated version really works for me and for the people I train. When I complete a profile for someone, it spans some 20 pages and includes what the person's motivators are, what their stressors are and how they are likely to interact with all other behaviour profiles. I use it like a 'sales bible' for most of the teams I train.

Julie French and Tony Burgess are not only very dear friends of mine, but also the experts, not only on this subject, but also in neurolinguistic programming and belief change. I highly recommend their training programmes.

– Chapter 12 –

How to introduce yourself and how to present yourself

We have already established that authenticity and personality are the two major keys in communicating well over the phone. This is the main reason that I don't believe in scripting verbatim. However, I do believe that you should spend time working out how to position your offering in the most appealing way. That will be discussed in more detail in the next chapter, whilst this one covers introducing yourself to your chosen contact.

This is not the pitch or presentation!

How to introduce yourself

There are five simple rules.

The rules of your introduction are:

1 Who you are
Some people think it's friendly to start by asking how that person is today, but without some form of introduction first, it has the opposite effect.

'Hello Michelle, how are you today?' is greeted with a 'Sorry, but *who* are you?' more often than not.

Using the warm call technique we discussed earlier, it should be something simple, such as, 'It's Michelle at Ethos.'

This should be followed by a positioning statement, for example, 'The chosen corporate caterers to…' a bit of a name drop never hurts, and it helps them if they can put you into a bit of a pigeon hole, too. Some people are afraid of this, but remember, if the contact can't recall you when he needs to, you will have lost out.

I learned this a long time ago, when I was trying to be everything to everyone, until I realised you have to allow yourself to be pigeon holed to a certain degree. I was Head of Client Development at a branding agency in London, and I had been nurturing a potential client for a while. I rang once to find out that this contact had placed several small jobs that we could have done.

'Oh, no! We could have done that for you!' I said, and he responded with,

'I'm so sorry, Michelle, I didn't realise you could do the smaller jobs, I only think of you for the bigger projects.' And I realised I had made our offering over complicated.

So I began to visualise my contacts with letter box shaped holes in their foreheads, and my delivery needed to fit into that letter box, otherwise they wouldn't be able to find it in the files of their minds when they needed to recall me.

That's followed by rule number two.

2 What you aim to achieve

This avoids getting to that stage of someone asking you to stop and tell them what you want, which has to be one of the worst things to happen.

It could be something like… 'I'm just calling to introduce myself and hope that we might have some common ground… I want to ensure I've got you registered correctly… I'm calling to see if you are aware of the funding available to your organisation,' or whatever works for your product/service.

By letting them know up front what you are trying to achieve, you show respect, confidence and integrity. It could even be something as bold as, 'I would love to have you on my client list, so I wanted to see how you like to be approached.'

3 Check that they are the ultimate decision maker

I prefer using the words 'in charge of' rather than 'responsible for', because 'responsible for' has connotations of being in trouble. 'Who's responsible for this mess?' so I might simply check by saying, 'You are ultimately in charge of personnel development, aren't you?' or, 'I am right in thinking that you are in charge of the utilities, aren't I?'

If they are not, then you should not go any further: you only present to the correct person. Find out who that is, and make your apologies, but if they could help you to reach that person, don't lose the opportunity. Get a direct telephone number, or find out when they are most likely to be in the office, and so on.

4 What you can do for them

It's a bugbear of mine when someone says, 'What I want is…' or, 'What I want to do…' because it's not *about you*. You are approaching someone out of the blue, and they will not want to hear about what you want to do. The emphasis has to be on how you can benefit them.

Whether that is saving costs, making profits, gaining recognition, or developing staff, it's all about benefiting the client. See Chapter 14 for Understanding Benefits and Features.

5 Ask permission!

As previously mentioned in the book, we should ask permission before proceeding any further. That's simply, 'Have I caught you at a good time?' or, 'Is it OK to talk now?'

Using your environmental listening skills, you may pick up that they are distracted or busy, in which case the words, 'Have I caught you in the middle of something?' are much more effective.

I have said this before, but you should not worry that you might be giving them the opportunity to make their excuses. You have to engage when it's right for them.

If they say that it's not a good time, then you ask when you can call back. Then, when you do call back, you are a 'warm' call. They are expecting you, they know who you are and they have given you permission.

How to present yourself

This is when you have permission to continue with your offering, and there are four rules.

1 Give the benefits

It might be a basic sales tool, but it amazes me how few sales people remember to focus on the client's needs.

In short, a benefit is the difference it will make to the client, and a feature is an aspect of your product or service.

As an example, if you were selling a torch, a benefit (to the client) would be that it enables them to see much better at night. Whereas a feature (of the product) might be that it is waterproof.

Too many people try to sell the features of the product, and forget about the benefits.

I was training someone new the other day, and in the first call I heard her make she didn't mention a single benefit to the client; instead she only presented the features of the product and the special deals that she could offer.

The effect can be very off putting. If it is not a two-way process, and you, as the client, can see nothing attractive in the product, then the subconscious suggestion is that no one is interested in it, which is why she's having to push it.

This is another example of how keeping your positioning strong and making your offer attractive works.

2 Share endorsements

It never hurts to share what other happy clients say about your product or service; it strengthens your case.

I always have a sheet of client endorsements in front of me when I am working on a new project, so I can refer to them whenever I need to. Sometimes it is appropriate to use competitor examples, and sometimes it is not, so make sure you know which is best under the circumstances.

Endorsements have been invaluable to me. It was back when I was an account manager working on the phones 20 years ago that I was first encouraged to gather them. I am one of the most recommended people on LinkedIn in the world now, and because my recommendations come from other people saying why they think I am good at what I do, I don't have to sell myself.

A recommendation from someone else is worth ten times what you could say yourself. Ensure you gather them when the opportunity is right. For me, that is when someone openly tells you that they had a great experience, that's the time to ask whether they would mind putting that in writing, because it would be so valuable to you.

I don't believe in fishing for them, or sending out requests for them, and a big 'no-no' to me is when someone asks you to write one yourself for them to sign. There is nothing genuine about that!

3 Give answers to objections

Understanding the difference between objections and fob-offs is essential.

An objection is the term used for someone giving you a reason why they don't want to buy, or don't want more information.

Objections are usually at decision maker level, and they require a response.

A fob-off is someone asking you to go away. Fob-offs are usually at reception level, and mean you need to do more homework.

> **Fob-offs – examples**
> It's a no name policy
> Sorry she's not available
> You will have to write in
> We can't put unsolicited calls through
> We're happy with our current supplier*

> **Objections – examples**
> All of those decisions are made at Head Office
> We have a three year contract
> We're happy with our current supplier*

(*This is on both lists, as it could be either a fob-off or an objection.)

Every objection you get should be answered, even if you have to go away and come back with an answer when you have the correct information.

You should never ask for the go-ahead without fully satisfying all the client's objections.

You may not be sure as to whether you are dealing with an objection or a fob-off, and I encourage you to ask in a straightforward manner, so you can handle it effectively.

Here are some examples of ways of understanding whether you are dealing with an objection or a fob-off.

Client: 'Can you call back in a month?'

You: 'Of course, I can. I don't want to waste your time, or mine, so is a month the right time for me to call back?'

Client: 'Can you put something in writing?'

You: 'Of course I can. What specifically do you want to see?' (Check interest and responsibility.)

In my experience, a high percentage of people who say they want to see something in writing are fobbing you off. A small percentage is made up of people who are very strong on detail, and want to see all the facts and figures. (These are usually our High 'C's' in DiSC® terms)

The remainder are a small percentage of people who are not the final decision makers and they might say, 'I just need something to give to the operations director.' That's proof that they are not going to make the decision themselves, so you need to disengage politely, and re-engage with the right person. 'Oh, I don't want you doing all the work…' or something to that effect.

If someone answers you with the words, 'I'm not interested,' your reaction should be one of slight surprise. Check whether it is their responsibility, and ask if there is a specific reason.

Many people assume that I must be 'thick skinned' because I use the phone so much in business and that could not be further from the truth. I am actually very sensitive. Those people are making assumptions that I am told to 'go away' a lot on the phone, and that I am used to being rejected. In fact, I'm not. People would usually only ask me to go away if I came across like a typical cold sales call.

The way that I learned to ensure that I don't face rejection an awful lot, was to design an objection handling technique which I call 'Pitch Inclusion'.

What that means is that I address the potential objections in my pitch. For example, if you suspect that your contact is the sort of person who would want to see the figures, (picked up through your use of DiSC® and VAKOG), you could pre-empt that objection with: 'I realise that someone in your position will want to see some corroborating figures, so I've taken the liberty of e-mailing you some over, which you should get in a second…'

The best way of dealing with an objection is to prevent it arising in the first place.

– Chapter 13 –

Closing

Closing is the term used for getting agreement to go ahead, and it's the main thing responsible for sales people having had a less than positive reputation.

Years ago, there were a number of closing techniques that were seen to work well. However, some were manipulative, some were pushy and some were just downright cheesy. Whether you believe that we have become more authentic in the way in which we communicate with each other, or whether you think it's simply because the majority of people in business now recognise strategies that have been in use for decades, one thing is certain; these closing techniques just don't work any more!

An effective close is as simple as asking, 'Would you like to go ahead with that?', or 'Shall I put you down for one?' or 'Is that something you would like to go ahead with?'

More contrived or 'strategic' phrases will immediately put you into the shoddy sales category. Defences will go up and phones will go down!

The shoddy salesman is the one that tries to close you every step of the way: 'So shall I put you down for one, or two?' before you have even had enough information to make a decision. And then, straight after your next question is answered, he tries to close you again. 'So, shall I get a pen so you can sign the order form?' It just makes him sound desperate, which in turn makes him sound unsuccessful. And no one wants to place business with someone who is unsuccessful.

There is just one rule that must be applied: you should never try to 'close' a potential client until you have answered every one of their questions. You can even check by asking, 'Did you have any other questions?' If they say no, then it's as good as saying yes to the sale, so that's when you confirm it with your close, 'Great, so would you like to go ahead with that then?'

Another phrase that I use is, 'Is there anything else you need from me before you make a decision?' If they say yes, then give them what they need. If they say no, then ask for the business with an authentic confirmation rather than a closing technique.

– Chapter 14 –

How to get a VIP to call you back and more voicemail message tips

Coaching on voicemail was something that I never used to include, because so few people used it, but as part of the evolution of the way in which we communicate, it is now very common.

More importantly, many people will now screen their calls, so they could well be listening to you while you leave your message, and be deciding whether to pick up.

It's important, therefore, to make it sound appealing or intriguing enough to entice them to return your call, whilst not being too evasive.

It always makes me quite cross when someone asks me to call them back if they want to sell to me, or if they want me to do something for them. It's the height of bad manners. If you are trying to get hold of them for your benefit, then it should be you doing the chasing.

It's like a romance; you woo the potential client, and that includes making 99% of the effort to reach them.

Where Phone Genius is concerned, there are six tips:

1) Say who you are and where you are from – in brief! (*not*, 'it's Michelle Mills-Porter from a company called…'. Remember the cold call versus warm call tips.)
2) How you can benefit them – in brief.
3) Be courteous about asking them to call you back. ('I thought you would like to know why I am trying to reach you, so in brief'… or… 'I wouldn't normally ask you to call me back, but I'm having difficulty reaching you'…)
4) Give them a really enticing reason why they should call you back.
5) Leave your details really clearly, and repeat your number as the very last thing.
6) Listen back to your voicemail! Most phone systems will give you the option now of listening back to your voicemail message, so once you have finished it, wait for the beep, then you should hear some options; to listen to it, to re-record it, to delete it, and so on.

This final tip has been a brilliant tool for me, as I have sometimes completely messed up a voicemail message, or rambled on, or got tongue tied. Listening back means that you don't have to worry; you can always re-record it. If you listen back to it, you can check whether you have left your number clearly enough and that you have used the toolbox correctly. Remember STOP!

However, my advice to you is that you should not re-record your message more than once!

Why?

Well, if they are screening their calls, you're going to sound a bit daft recording and re-recording the same thing! Ha! You will be the office joke by the end of the day!

And, of course, a good sprinkling of personality is the magic ingredient to make the voicemail come alive!

I was working with a catering company, 'Britain's', that provided sample lunches for their potential clients, so that was an easy offering and a delight to work with.

As part of our voicemail message we might use, 'Hi, it's Michelle here at Britain's, and I wondered if you would like to have lunch? My treat!'

Or an even cheekier version, 'Aw, voicemail, that's ruined my heartfelt proposal somewhat!'

Along the same theme, '… and as you are the person ultimately in charge of the gastronomic experience of your VIP guests, I chose you to be my lunch date.'

If you can get your personality across in the voicemail message, then you have a very good chance of building a relationship.

Nobody has ever told me that they wouldn't do business with me because I am unprofessional, and, as long as you take into consideration the industry nuances, you stand a good chance of making far more friends than you do of people who don't care for your style. But, as Pete Freeman taught me, there is a percentage of people out there who are not going to like you, and there's nothing you can do about that. Just concentrate on the ones that you get on with.

– Chapter 15 –

My hot tips

Getting through an automated telephone system

Automated phone systems can be a nightmare. You can go round and round without speaking to a single person for ages. Sometimes they give you no option to talk to anyone at all, and that can be soul destroying.

Here are a couple of tips that may help you to get off the merry-go-round. First, try pressing the hash key when it is not a given option. Sometimes, maybe on the second or third attempt, the system might pick it up as being a call that is incompatible with the system, as your options are not being recognised, and it could divert you directly to a real person to talk with instead.

You could also try dialling zero even if it's not an option, and sometimes this is a fast track to reception.

If you are really stuck, and nothing else is working try changing the last two digits of the phone number, and that might get you through to an actual person's extension rather than the main number. Extension numbers tend to be the same number to start with, but with different digits at the end, whether that be the last three or four numbers. So, if the reception number ends with 200, you might try 210, or any number you fancy, and see if it's still the same company. If it is indeed the same company, then I apologise, and say that I wanted the marketing department, or whichever one I wanted to get though to.

The deadly pregnant pause

The pregnant pause is for use when you need information, or are trying to get through, and you are not getting a positive response. It is only to be used when building rapport is not important.

When used correctly it can have a very powerful effect!

It can be used to coax someone into giving you more information, because it gives an air of expectation. 'Can you tell me who is ultimately in charge of personnel development, please?'

'Well it's someone in the human resources…'

If you want to make its effect more gentle then you can add an acknowledging noise or a small 'Yes?…'

I use it when I have not received an adequate answer.

This is when I call it a deadly pregnant pause.

My husband says he can always tell when someone is in trouble on the other end of the phone, as I start to enunciate precisely, I drop the tone and pace of my voice and, as he says, I sound like Dame Margaret Thatcher! If he hears me giving a deadly pregnant pause, (in other words, he can hear that they have said something and I haven't responded) he gets out of the office quick smart!

Imagine that I am speaking with a customer care department, and I am having a heated conversation. The customer care advisor says to me, 'So what exactly do you want me to do about it?'

Then the pregnant pause! Say nothing, and it is more powerful than anything at all! It leaves an overwhelming silence which needs to be filled, and an awkwardness that will make them want to fill it with something… He who breaks the silence, loses!

OK, so that's a bit dramatic, but I have used it with great effect in lots of situations, and at the very least it can make someone think, 'Did I come across in the way I wanted to then? Was I as helpful as I could have been?'

The final call

Probably the hottest tip I can give anyone, the final call. This has worked wonders for me over the years, and it has had VIPs from some of the most prestigious companies in the world calling me back almost immediately.

This is for use when you have built great rapport with someone, and you are at the critical stage of sealing the deal, whatever that may be. You can't seem to reach them, and all you can get is their voicemail.

Now is the time for you to leave your final call.

This is when you tell them you are not going to call again.

(You are breaking it off!)

The way you deliver it is, of course, the key to its effectiveness.

The way that I deliver it is like this.

Start with:

'I realise you must be up against it'… (or 'I realise I must have slipped down the priority list'… or… 'I realise something must have come up'…).

Followed by:

'And I don't want to be a pain in the neck,' (or I don't want to become a nuisance,' or 'I don't want to chase you.')

Then with:

'So this is my final call.' (Or 'I won't be calling you again.' Or 'I won't keep leaving messages, this is the last one.')

And finished with:

'So, if you still want to talk, please call me, on my direct line…'

(Or 'However, I will be here for you as soon as you need me, here's my personal direct line…' or 'So I'm leaving the ball in your court, so just call me on…')

I've had people call me back with, 'Oh! Michelle, I'm so sorry, you are on my priority list, I've just been so busy…' and 'I felt awful when I got your message, I've just been waiting on budgets.'

So it seems that, if you have built a good relationship, then they will call you back, and usually they will feel a bit bad about having left it for so long, too.

This one tip alone has brought more decisions to fruition than I can remember. Use it well!

– Afterword –

And now the time has come for us to part (though not for long, I hope).

I hope you've been able to apply the strategies and tips to your own situations and that Phone Genius will make a difference in the effectiveness of how you use the phone.

Remember the two key elements are authenticity and personality and everything else is cream on top.

Referring to my own advice, if you want to make a real change, then practise the most important elements of Phone Genius for 28 days consecutively. (You can have weekends off!) Then you should have formed new habits and if you continue to practise these elements, you have every chance of them becoming subconscious activities.

So whether you use the phone for customer care, or for marketing, or selling, research or fundraising, is it worth 28 days of practise for you to be rewarded with great rapport building skills, conquering of your fears and a renewed confidence? Great results?

No matter how you use the phone, if you apply what I have shared with you, you can become a Phone Genius.

Phone Genius is delivered in in-house training programmes that help teams to implement new strategies as they take them on board, and it can be tailored to suit senior sales teams, account management teams, customer care teams, or mixed teams in a small hands on organisation.

I'd be glad to help in any way I can. So please connect with me in any way you like – just connect.

uk.linkedin.com/in/michellemillsporter
www.ethosdevelopmentltd.co.uk
phonegenius@ethosdevelopmentltd.co.uk

– Acknowledgements –

'Acknowledgements' does not do justice to most of the people I mention in this book.

Please let me show my appreciation to some very important people, most of whom have been mentioned in this book, in alphabetical order. (first name):

Daniel Kish MA, MA – President, World Access for the Blind
www.worldaccessfortheblind.org
'An absolute inspiration.'

Darren Moore – talented portrait photographer
http://www.darrenmoorephotography.co.uk

Drew Montague – fine wine investment specialist
www.montaguefinewines.com
'My good friend and confidant.'

Ellie Rich – graphic designer, www.ellierichdesign.com
'The mother of the Phone Monsters.'

Gary Vey – Editor of Viewzone, www.viewzone.com
'Bold, controversial and important'.

Jenny Maxwell – multiple best-selling author, MD of Water Alert
'The first run through editor of *Phone Genius*, "mad as a box of frogs" and beloved friend.'

Jon Holland – founder and CEO of Eternol Design Studios
'The designer of the Phone Genius logo and book cover, talented and rare designer.'

Jon and Jay Rixon – Directors, Lansalot Ltd, www.lansalot.co.uk
'Treasured friends and celebrated geeks.'

Jude Jennison – MD, Leaders By Nature, www.leadersbynature.com
'Lovely friend and enlightened trainer.'

Dr Julien Doyon PhD – Scientific Director, Functional Neuroimaging Unit University of Montreal. Director Quebec Bio-Imaging Network.

Pete Freeman – executive coach, www.freemancoaching.co.uk
'Important friend and my sage advisor.'

Martin Rhodes MSc MBA FCMI – performance improvement specialist
Martin@coachcasebook.com
'Important friend and brilliant coach.'

Neil Hillman MPSE – free-range sound designer, re-recording mixer, location recordist and outside broadcast sound supervisor.
www.theaudiosuite.com
'Authority on all things audio and lovely friend.'

Peter Thomson – The UK's most prolific information product creator
www.peterthomson.com
'My earliest mentor and important influence.'

Rob Boylett – CEO BP&N, www.bpnetworks.co.uk
'Trusted associate and expert.'

Sue Richardson – Sue Richardson Associates Ltd, suerichardson.co.uk
'Lovely friend and *Phone Genius* publisher.'

Tony Burgess and **Julie French** – Directors of Academy of High Achievers Ltd, www.aha-success.com
'Dear friends and bringers of light.'

– About the author –

Michelle is a leading authority in the field of communication over the phone.

She has a proven track record of building successful relationships using just the phone, having worked with directors at Microsoft, Disney, GlaxoSmithKline, Texaco, BT, several premiership football clubs and many leading UK entrepreneurs.

While continuing to execute successful business development projects on behalf of her clients, Michelle also runs training programmes for in-house teams as well as apprenticeships and highly sought-after workshop programmes.

Michelle's intention is to work with as many people as possible to give them the ability to apply the science of Phone Genius to excel in their communication over the phone.

Michelle is also a recognised Global Networking Giant, speaker, trainer, consultant and one of the most recommended people on LinkedIn across the globe.

http://www.ethosdevelopmentltd.co.uk/what-is-phone-genius/